The Editor Makes House Calls

Secrets of Being Published

by

Allison Mitcham
and
Yvonne Wilson

DREAMCATCHER PUBLISHING
Saint John • New Brunswick • Canada

DreamCatcher Publishing acknowledges the support of the New Brunswick
Arts Council. We acknowledge the support of the Government of Canada
through the Book Publishing Industry Development Program (BPIDP) for
our publishing activities.

Canadian Cataloguing in Publication Data

Mitcham, Allison - 1932

Wilson, Yvonne - 1927

The Editor Makes House Calls - Secrets of Being Published

ISBN - 1-894372-26-3
            1. Authorship. I. Wilson, Yvonne, 1927- II. Title.
      PN153.M58 2003 808'.02   C2003-903640-5

Some names have been changed to protect privacy.

Typesetter: Chas Goguen

Cover Design: Dawn Drew, INK Graphic Design Services Corp.

Printed and bound in Canada

DREAMCATCHER PUBLISHING INC.
1 Market Square
Suite 306 Dockside
Saint John, New Brunswick, Canada E2L 4Z6
www.dreamcatcher.nb.ca

Acknowledgements

The authors have to thank Elizabeth Margaris, our publisher, for the idea that we might collaborate on this project, and for the fun we had converting her idea into a book.

But our heart-felt gratitude is reserved for Chas Goguen, Elizabeth's Executive Assistant, who designed the chapters. His accuracy, eye for balance and harmony, and his attention to detail, all applied patiently and cheerfully, made putting this book together an extension of the fun we had writing it.

Dawn Drew, who designed the cover, is also wonderful to work with and her cover has our enthusiastic endorsement.

We also have to thank Lafe Locke for the title.

Allison and Yvonne

For our daughters

Kate and Lucy Wilson

and

Stephanie Mitcham

scientists who write lucid English prose

and

Naomi Mitcham

who paints like an angel

Other Works by Yvonne Wilson

Of novels for adult readers:

Red Dragon Square

Of novels for children:

Slipper Hbr.
A Light Above the Sun

Among other writers' works edited to publication:

Overtime   by Brad Janes
The Making of Harry Cossaboom
            by Jerrod Edson
Dancing With the Dead
            by Vernon Oickle
To Hell or Melbourne and
Until We Meet Again
            by Flora Kidd
The World That Is
            by Alan Weatherley
Strange Lights at Midnight
            by Allison Mitcham
A Wolf to Remember
            by Kali Brazier-Tompkins
Saint John Vocational School - in Retrospect
            by Faye Somers
By Invitation Only
            by Gail Higgins
Locked In Locked Out
            by Shawn Jennings

Other Works by Allison Mitcham

Strange Lights at Midnight, a novel, DreamCatcher Publishing, 2003.

A Little Boy Catches a Whale, children's book, 2002. Adaptation of the Mi'kmaq (Indian) tale from Silas Rand's transcription. The book has translations in French and Mi'kmaq and watercolor illustrations opposite every story page by the author's daughter, Naomi. Published by Bouton d'or.

Angels in the Snow, a novel, Crane Creek (USA), 2000.

Maritime Voices, a collection of short stories including one of Mitcham's, co-edited with Dr. Theresia Quigley, DreamCatcher Publishing, 2000.

Meat Goats, (with Stephanie Mitcham, D.V.M.), Crane Creek Publications, 2000.

Poetic Voices of the Maritimes: a Selection of Contemporary Poetry, (co-edited with Theresia Quigley) Lancelot Press, 1996.

Taku, Heart of North America's Last Great Wilderness, illustrated by Naomi and Peter Mitcham, Lancelot Press, 1993. Won the British Columbia Lieutenant Governor's Medal in 1994.

Grey Owl's Favorite Wilderness Revisited, Penumbra, 1991. (Distributed by University of Toronto Press and subsequently by General Publishing.)

Atlin, the Last Utopia: subarctic outpost and portal to the land of eagle, wolf and grizzly (non-fiction study of the outpost mentality), illustrated by Naomi Mitcham, Lancelot Press, 1989. (Second printing, 1992; third printing, 1994.)

Island Keepers (biography and non-fiction study of the outpost mentality), Lancelot Press, 1989. (Second printing, 1990; third printing, 1993.)

Paradise or Purgatory: island life in Nova Scotia and New Brunswick (non-fiction study of the outpost mentality and regional folklore), Lancelot Press, 1986, (Second printing, 1987; third printing, 1994.) Illustrated by Peter Mitcham.

Numerous articles and poems in magazines, periodicals, and books.

What her writers say about Yvonne Wilson as editor:

I had finished writing my memoirs - eventually published as *Locked In Locked Out* - and realised it was now time to show my finished work to an editor. I was shy to have anyone read my manuscript, especially an editor. I had never written before. Would she laugh at my grammar? Throw it in the trash? Infer that I was presumptuous to think I could write with little training?

Yvonne Wilson did none of these things; instead she was positive and supportive. She implied to me: grammar was important, but the story, style, and tone were paramount. She made a novice writer like me feel welcomed into the literary world. She guides a writer, rather than dictates. Yvonne Wilson, as an editor, is a gentle hand.

> *Shawn Jennings, M.D.*
> *Locked In Locked Out*
> *Formerly a family physician*

I met Yvonne Wilson when I was thirteen and seeking a publisher for my first novel. I was terrified. She seemed so forbidding, and she had to be infinitely more intelligent than I. How on earth was I going to make a good impression? Once my hands stopped shaking, though, I learned that I had nothing to fear. Yvonne is soft-spoken and very astute in her judgement. Her critical eye misses little, and you can be sure she isn't going to mellow anything she has to say for the sake of sensitive feelings, though her indefatigable wit makes the criticism much easier to swallow.

Yvonne is a great editor. She doesn't demand changes; she 'suggests' changes. A lot of them. Then she gives the work back to be pored over and edited appropriately. She always makes it clear, though, that it would be in your best interests to make the changes she's suggested.

I haven't worked with many editors and I have no way to rank Yvonne on an editor-of-the-year scale, but I *can* say that it has been a pleasure to work with her these past few years. Her support and encouragement - along with several small novels detailing the finer points of grammar on the backs of successive manuscripts - have brought me into the publishing world.

> *Kali Brazier-Tompkins*
> *A Wolf to Remember*
> *Student*

Yvonne edits with ruthless and remorseless gentle persuasion, and with the prescience to see through the dross and incoherence of draft to the essential narrative. She hasn't been 'just' an editor for me; she's also been a demanding, precise and meticulous writing *teacher*.

Robert M. Rayner
The Ragged Believers
Educator

In the short time I have known Yvonne Wilson I have learned that she has all the attributes that make a good editor. Teacher, author of four fiction books, world traveller, reader and student of literature she is strict about correct grammar, punctuation, and spelling but always objective in her consideration and judgement of the content and writing style of the works brought to her attention. The range is wide and varied from romantic novels to moralistic accounts of the state of the planet, stories for children and personal memoirs of pain and suffering. With a kind of gentle wisdom Yvonne points out to authors where to delete unnecessary sentences, paragraphs and chapters or to expand and develop characters so that the message the writer wishes to send to readers is comprehensible as well as entertaining.

It is only right and proper that to assist would-be writers wanting to be published Yvonne and Allison Mitcham have collected together and presented in this book their combined knowledge and experience of the problems that all writers face when seeking to have their work published. At last New Brunswick writers will have the benefit of advice on how to write and get published from two of their own successful authors of literature.

Flora Kidd
Author of over 60 novels

Yvonne has been my editor for about three years. Although at times she can be a bit unyielding, her guidance and patience have taught me to be a better writer. I wouldn't trade that for the world.

John Codner
John's first book of short stories is to be published in 2004
Journalist

Unlike many editors, whose function seems to be merely to criticize, Yvonne Wilson is a true teacher who does more than improve a manuscript. She improves the author too, and does so in an accepting, encouraging manner that gives one confidence. In my tentative transition from non-fiction to novels, I could not have been more fortunate than to have her guide my efforts.

Peter H. Riddle
Running Away
Professor of Music, Acadia University

Yvonne Wilson excels as an editor of fiction in getting authors to stick to the main thrust of their stories by persuading them to jettison irrelevant characters, scenes and side issues, tighten narrative structure and do all they can to maintain their own interest and passion in the characters and situations they are inventing. She understands how story continuity can and must be maintained and where climaxes should occur - and she pays relentless attention to these matters. She can be argued with but, in my experience, her judgements, though not necessarily easy to accept, are nearly always right. She is also extremely effective in the nuts and bolts matters of editing - such as spelling and basic grammar.

I have found Yvonne Wilson firm - not very yielding - in her editing but, though somewhat stubborn myself, I usually take her advice because, on mature reflection about what she has said, I am nearly always persuaded she is right. I consider myself extremely lucky to have had the benefits of her intelligence, insight and meticulousness. I am sure that *The Editor Makes House Calls*, which she has co-authored with Allison Mitcham, will prove to be of outstanding value to all authors, whether first-timers or more seasoned performers.

Alan Weatherley
Professor emeritus, University of Toronto
Novelist and Painter of landscapes

A gifted writer in her own right, Ms. Wilson generously shares her talents with aspiring writers who have the good fortune to have her as an editor. She has taught me well, always patient, always willing to explain something in as many different ways as needed until I have understood. My first novel was an interesting concept. Wilson has helped me make it a cohesive and "can't-put-it-down" (I hope!) story. She has taught me to waltz amidst the Wedgwood, whereas previously I was a bear in a china shop. (No bull....)

Marci Lin Melvin
Nova Scotia lawyer and author

As a first time author I felt truly blessed to have Yvonne Wilson as my editor. While respecting my decisions, her gentle suggestions and attention to detail consistently improved my book. Her grasp of the content and my struggle to clarify an idea brought forth solutions which were sometimes brilliant. Our time together was enlightening, productive and fun.

Gail Higgins
By Invitation Only
Poet

A special thank you goes to Yvonne Wilson and Elizabeth Margaris for taking me in off the street and showing me the ropes. Your energy levels are amazing.

Brad Janes
Overtime
Journatlist/Novelist

RE: *The Best of Alden Nowlan*, Lancelot Press, 1993

For those unfamiliar with Nowlan's work, Mitcham's concise introduction is generous and shrewd. For the initiated, her selection is a sentimental journey into one person's "best" of Nowlan.

> E.L. Edmonds
> *Canadian Book Review Annual, 1993*

RE: *Maritime Voices*, DreamCatcher Publishing, 2000

It is wonderful that these gems have been saved for posterity by two professors of English at the Université de Moncton, Allison Mitcham and Theresia Quigley.

> Kate Rutherford
> "The New Brunswick Reader," *Saint John Telegraph Journal*, February 10, 2001

RE: *Poetic Voices of the Maritimes*, edited by Allison Mitcham and Theresia Quigley, Lancelot Press, 1996

As the editors note, the book aims to provide for the 1990s what Cockburn and Gibbs's *Ninety Seasons: Modern Poems from the Maritimes* (1974) and Fred Cogswell's *Atlantic Anthology* (1985) provided for earlier decades. It achieves its purpose. The standard is, in general, high... This is an attractive anthology, both as a text for schools and universities and as a book for anyone who is interested in the art of poetry.

> W.J. Keith
> *Canadian Book Review Annual, 1996*

The book [*Offshore Islands of Nova Scotia and New Brunswick*]... offers also a special bonus: the superb art work of Peter Mitcham, the author's husband, a teacher, writer, and imaginative illustrator.

Harold T. Shea
Halifax Chronicle-Herald, August 7, 1984

Her book [*Taku*] is richly illustrated with photographs from Alaskan and Canadian archives, with watercolors by her daughter [Naomi], and with ink drawings by her husband [Peter].

Barry M. Gough
Canadian Book Review Annual, 1993

"The fine black-and-white drawings by Peter Mitcham create interest in the stories [in *Offshore Islands of Nova Scotia and New Brunswick*] and serve to indicate where these islands are located.

Susanne Day
Canadian Book Review Annual, 1995

COAUTHORED BOOKS

Coauthored books are uncommon for lots of reasons.

First of all, it's unlikely that you'll find someone in your family or among your friends and acquaintances who not only wants to write a book with you, but is able to do just that. If by chance you do come across such a rare person, he or she should be a proven and published author, as you yourself must be.

Besides, undertaking such a venture is not just a matter of willingness and capability, but of personality. Coauthoring means cooperation of the most intensive kind. The two authors need to be on the same frequency with both the subject of the book and the approach to be taken. They must also agree on the time frame. Your project is doomed if you churn out a chapter or so every week, and your would-be partner's interest flags to the extent that he or she offers up only a few pages every six months or so.

Then too, there's the matter of temperament: some people are difficult to work with, no matter what. So if cooperation in any capacity is not their long suit, one should realize before embarking on a project that coauthoring a book with such an individual is out of the question.

Coauthoring is not an undertaking for beginning writers. Both authors need to have proven themselves. Although an amateur might suppose that writing a book with someone else is a lot easier than writing one by oneself, this is probably not the case.

For instance, I know of two would-be writers - girls in their early twenties - enrolled in a friend's creative writing course some years ago - who decided to write a Harlequin romance jointly. Neither had written anything much before, certainly not for publication. Still, they thought writing this book would be a breeze. Not so.

Apparently, they didn't get beyond the first chapter, which they tried to work on together, orally, by recording what they said as they went along. Moreover, according to what my teacher-friend told me, neither girl had an overall plan for the book. Another major problem was that their styles didn't mesh. Small wonder their joint project fizzled out!

This example raises the point that fiction - even a Harlequin romance - is rarely a suitable genre for a cooperative venture. That goes for poetry as well. Both are too much the product of the individual mind and heart.

Books which sometimes are effectively co-authored are works of non-fiction, particularly of the 'how-to' or 'self-help' variety. I've had experience with three books of this type - with happy results. With such books, the combined experiences of the authors can prove more valuable and illuminating than the know-how of a single writer - even a very well-informed one who holds forth in a lucid and persuasive style.

The first two books I helped write were animal books, which my veterinary pathologist daughter, turned farmer, suggested.

The first was The Angora Goat. Angoras, whose homeland is Turkey (near Ankara, formerly called Angora), are famous for their luxurious and durable hair - mohair. At the time of writing this book, Stephanie had more than a hundred of these exceptional animals, whose attributes I had had opportunities to observe during a number of lengthy visits at kidding time. Still, goats of any kind were not creatures I had ever, in my wildest dreams, anticipated writing about.

However, Stephanie was persuasive. She would

write the medically-based chapters, as well as the practical how-to parts about housing and feeding the animals. She had all these facts at her fingertips. Besides, she is that rare scientist who can write well, having published pieces in the popular as well as the scientific press.

My part of the book entailed researching and writing about the history of these special animals and the extraordinary qualities of mohair. To my surprise, this turned out to be a fascinating assignment. I was especially interested in the Turks' fondness for these animals, and the attributes of mythic scope attributed to them by residents in the countryside surrounding Ankara.

By the time I tackled my part of this project I had researched and written ten factual books and scads of articles, so I was not daunted by the prospect of researching and writing on a new subject. And, since Stephanie and I have always worked exceptionally well together, compatibility in co-authoring this work was not a problem.

We were also very fortunate in that my then long-time publisher, Bill Pope of Lancelot Press, agreed even before the book was finished to publish it as soon as we completed the manuscript. He said that, since none of my earlier books had flopped, he didn't expect this one to. It didn't!

The first edition of The Angora Goat went through two printings - the initial print run, chiefly because Stephanie had so many contacts who were interested in the book. Subsequently, it sold internationally, and, when last we heard, it was being translated into Danish.

Shortly before the second printing sold out, Stephanie and I decided we needed to bring out a new, enlarged edition. We had gradually been accumulating additional material - about 100 pages more, in fact. This edition is still in print.

By the late nineties, Stephanie and I had already begun another goat book, Meat Goats. Goat meat, chevon, is a preferable alternative to beef - much healthier and hugely better for the environment, facts which much of the rest of the world has long been aware of but many North Americans are just learning. Stephanie and I once more divided up the research and writing according to our tastes and abilities. So far, this book, published in 2000, has had rave reviews and been even more successful than The Angora Goat.

The third coauthored book I have been involved with is this one, The Editor Makes House Calls. It was the idea of Yvonne Wilson and Elizabeth Margaris, editor and publisher, repectively, of DreamCatcher Publishing. I was invited to contribute.

The circumstances seemed auspicious. Both Yvonne and I had had a lot of experience writing, editing and teaching - not always similar experiences, it is true, but that has been a good thing as far as widening the book's scope. Then too, Yvonne and I felt we could work well together. We have similar objectives and we like each other. As when Stephanie and I collaborated, Yvonne and I have each written separate portions of this work, pieces which have meshed easily.

Finally, neither one of us was going to let grass grow under our feet. We had a deadline: we would stick to it.

And best of all, this book had a ready readership. Orders for the book began to flow in even before it went to press. All this goes to show that under the very best circumstances coauthoring can work.

Introduction

Carl Senna

Author, editorial writer and columnist

Teacher of writing

Ever since literature became big business, which for many scholars dates from the 19th century, commercial and artistic motives have coexisted in a kind of creative tension, for the market for books has had to be developed and the expectations of the market have had to be served on a regular basis. That has meant rules, formats, and the cultivation of tastes in writing. Successful authors therefore have had need of skilled editors as coaches, mentors and collaborators, so much so that an entire school of criticism has derided the very notion of authorship, to confuse, in Northrop Frye's phrase, "imaginative with discursive writing." To quote the authors, Allison Mitcham and Yvonne Wilson, of *The Editor Makes House Calls: Secrets of Being Published*, "Writing is Art... Publishing is Business... And the Partnership is Uneasy." Editing, that is, like the process of publishing itself, is not authorship. And only a fool, to paraphrase the old saw about serving as one's own lawyer, would trust what he writes to publication without the services of an editor.

The point is that the most difficult kind of writing - some might say the kind of effort that leads to writer's block or, better, writer's procrastination - is whenever one simultaneously attempts to edit oneself in the act of writing. Every author has to get it written before he or she tries to get it right, for editors may only refine and polish writing that has actually been written, rather than consider the idea of the work still in the author's imagination which he or she has put off in the future to write. But just as no serious athlete nor professional performer would both train and coach him-or-herself, for the two skills involve the critically necessary element of different points of view - one to perform one's intention, the other to gauge how well the actual performance accomplishes the goal - serious writing is seldom finished without the trained intervention of an editor to achieve its meaning and its effect.

The legendary editor Maxwell Perkins (who edited F. Scott Fitzgerald, Ernest Hemingway, Thomas Wolfe, Ring Lardner, J.P. Marquand, Edmund Wilson, Marjorie Kinnan Rawlings, Sherwood Anderson, James Jones, Alan Paton, Taylor Caldwell, Nancy Hale, and many other distinguished authors) told a group of his New York University extention students a year before he died: "an editor does not add to a book. At best he serves as a handmaiden to an author. Don't ever get to feeling important about yourself, because an editor at most releases energy. He creates nothing."

Allison Mitcham and Yvonne Wilson fulfill the philosophy of Perkins of the editor as both guide and catalyst. The text of this highly readable handbook of insights offers candid bits of wisdom, interspersed with writing anecdotes, encouragement, and editing scenarios from the arcane world of book publishing. For prospective new authors in search of publishers, there will be few books so valuable or timely as this one. Essay chapters alternate in separate but complementary narratives, instructive commentary, episodes and illustrations by either Mitcham or Wilson jointly. Here readers will discover little known general expectations of commercial publishers and agents of authors, particularly the kind of necessary submission guidelines for unpublished authors.

This is a book of modest length, but it is filled with gems of wisdom from lifetimes of writing and editorial experiences. It will save many beginning authors much time and grief in obtaining a publisher. For Mitcham, a former English professor and award-winning author, is the author of 30 books, in fiction, poetry and non-fiction categories. The Sackville, New Brunswick, author has had a number of commercial successes published. Her collaborator in *The Editor Makes House Calls*, Yvonne Wilson is Acquisitions Editor of DreamCatcher Publishing, in Saint John, New Brunswick, as well as author of non-fiction and fiction. Both are teachers of writing, and in Mitcham's case, she has been a distinguished Professor of Literature as well. Together they follow the path of self-effacing editors, each, to quote again the inimitable Perkins, as "a little dwarf on the shoulder of a great general advising him what to do and what not to do, without anyone's noticing."

This is a wise, wittily composed book, easy to read, humorous and it offers beginning writers many practical applications of its lessons.

(Carl Senna, the author of *Colin Powell: A Man of War and Peace* (NY: Walker, 1992), and several other books, is an editorial writer and columnist, having written for *The New York Times Sunday Magazine*, *The Sunday Times Book Review*, *The Boston Globe*, *The Christian Science Monitor*, and other American and international newspapers. He has worked both for Beacon Press and Schenkman Publishing as an acquisition editor, as an editorial writer for Allyn & Bacon Company, and he has taught writing at Harvard University, Tufts University, Providence College, and the Universities of Rhode Island and Massachusetts at Boston, among others. He lives now in Saint John, New Brunswick.)

Table of Contents

Chapter Four:
Clarity, Unity, Euphony 77

Chapter Five:
My MS has been accepted by a publisher. I have a letter of intent; a contract will follow. 106

Chapter Six:
The Reasons Why
Why we must promote ourselves and our work and some ways to do it 147

Chapter Seven:
Well, Then, How DO I Write, Anyway? 161

Section A: Setting up to Write 162

CHAPTER ONE:

MY MANUSCRIPT IS FINISHED.

WHAT DO I DO NOW?

First Readers:

First Readers are those close friends and relations who read your story in manuscript. They're wonderful. They LOVE your story. They LOVE you. They LOVE being the first to read the next winner of the Governor-General's Prize. But unless they're retired professors of creative writing, don't trust their judgment. And never, ever let them near your editor or publisher.

Choose your First Readers warily.

"*You* are writing a book? You must need your head read!"

Don't choose that one, even if she's your troublesome sister-in-law. Crawl under the table and hide (with your manuscript) whenever she comes into the room. Don't let her sniff out even a whiff of your story, because...

She makes you feel.........................

(enter reply here)

If you need a hint, choose from our partial list:

apprehensive		petrified
breathless	indignant	queasy
confident	joyful	raring to go
determined	kind (to dumb animals)	superior
ebullient	lethal	terrified
forgiving	magnanimous	unshakeable
grouchy	nervous	victorious
happy	outraged	weak in the knees

Add your own contribution to the list if you like.

But be honest.

If your choices fall among the negatives, you maybe *should* see a psychiatrist - for help in overcoming the tenderness of your feelings; to build up your confidence.

If your choices suggest overconfidence, beware. You may be in for a shock. Better submit to a revealing "head-read" right away, to be sure your arrogance isn't terror in disguise.

My favourite writers are determined but flexible; a little nervous at our first meeting; confident, but ready to hear my side of the story; and probably about forty years old.

Alberta dropped in one wintry day, unsnapped her parka, and drew out of protective custody the manuscript (MS) of a novel that met DreamCatcher's criteria: Atlantic-Canadian author, story set in the Maritimes, on a theme that interested us...

Alberta and I worked together for about a year, till the MS was ready for publication. Then DreamCatcher placed the story on the list for the *next* year. But the next year turned out to be the year of the Chapters debacle, when the book publishing industry in Canada staggered to its knees under the weight of losses. Among others - many others, Canada-wide - Alberta's book was bumped to the list for the *following* year.

But Alberta lost her nerve. She withdrew her book. She had every right to do so, and the publisher surrendered the MS without a contentious word. ***But, Alberta honey, every other book that was on the list with yours is now in print.***

THINGS HAPPEN.
HANG IN and HANG ON.

Alberta sent a first reader to pick up her MS.

Ratcheting her voice to an angry squeak, Alberta's friend couldn't understand why we had changed our plans for her friend's stupendous book.

Thousands of dollars we couldn't collect, for example?

But Alberta's friend wasn't listening. We should be held responsible, and she was just the little girl to tell us so.

We *were* being held responsible. The landlord, the phone company, the stationer, the graphics designer, the courier service... the lot of them were holding us responsible. We were supposed to publish books with thin air? That was all we were collecting from our distributor.

But Alberta's friend wasn't listening.

Then there was Ivry who sent us a MS we couldn't use. I read it carefully, called Ivry - she lived in another town - and we discussed her story. I made a few suggestions for improvement. Ivry understood what I meant, said she would consider some changes, and sounded as if she was taking her rejection very well.

But Ivry, too, sent a first reader to pick up her MS.

Yes, you're right. As her face grew redder and redder, Ivry's friend couldn't understand why we wouldn't want Ivry's story. It was just what the world needed. It was a thing of beauty, of pure and unsullied spirituality, the child of genius...

Dear First Reader,

Publishers receive many more manuscripts (MSS) than they can ever bring out as books, and turn down many more sight unseen.

You may be right in your judgement of the quality of your friend's work, but publishers deal with distributors, who, in turn, deal with book sellers. The distributors know what sorts of books their sellers want and what sorts their publishers are producing.

A's books, for example - non-fiction, illustrated, hockey perhaps - go to seller B, who has a shop in the arena, and they do well. Now suppose A slips in a slushy romance for love-starved widows of sixty. That would be like the time we found a coral snake in the bananas.

Yours very truly,
    The Ac. Ed.

Writers:

Love your first readers: appreciate them, let them read your stories and gush over them. But deal with your publisher yourself. We know your abusive friends are really very nice people who are only terribly disappointed for you, their friend who writes such wonderful stories. They don't understand that we hate turning people down, that often we feel just as bad as you do - and your friends - but that we are trying to run a business.

WRITING IS ART

PUBLISHING IS BUSINESS

AND THE PARTNERSHIP IS UNEASY

Agents:

Your friends have read your book, your parents are busting the buttons right off their vests, your spouse is dreaming of a new car, and your kids are planning a trip to Disney World. Something has to be done.

This is the time for you to go to the library and consult reference lists for suitable agents and publishers.

Note: **SUITABLE**

If you have skimmed through this book, you have guessed by now that maybe not every agent is going to be thrilled with your novel based on the life of Wilf Carter; not every publisher will wait with baited breath for your handbook on raising koalas in a sunny corner of your basement – with or without photographs.

But you remember the new car, the trip to Disney World, and persevere.

Who are these literary agents anyway?

What do they do?

What might one do for you?

In a word, WHAT ARE THEY FOR?

The plain truth is this:

We writers are artists whose creations are very close to our (often tender) hearts.

We can be egotistical, unreasonable, volatile; and publishers often have to break - at least bruise - our tender feelings.

Our first readers are partisans who will carry on guerrilla warfare with "their" author's "so-called" editor and publisher, both face to face and behind unguarded backs.

> **Many publishers, therefore, protect themselves from writers and their friends by dealing only with agents.**

Last time I enquired, Harlequin would talk directly to writers; most other "name" publishers would not.

BUT

Well connected agents, who can make lucrative deals for writers, are as hard to reach and to interest in your work as publishers are.

Also, agents - good or bad - assuming you can find one, take a slice (generally 15%) of what you make. Not what the publisher makes - **what you make.**

> **Most unknown writers, therefore, have to give up dreams of the big name, the famous logo, and settle for a small publishing house where somebody in authority still answers the phone.**

ALLISON SAYS:

Finding a publisher is frequently no easy task - unless you are a celebrity or your subject, on which you are the recognized and televised authority, is particularly timely and preferably controversial. Yet you'd never guess this on first perusing publishers' directories. Looking through such tomes, the aspiring author seems to have plenty of choices - that is, until he looks closely at the stipulations set out under each press's heading.

For instance, most of the big publishers state categorically at the end of their blurb that they receive no unsolicited manuscripts. So right away that avenue is blocked, unless you have an inside track or can find a good agent, someone who can interest an editor enough to get your manuscript past the door and read promptly and thoughtfully.

And if you pick an agent blindly from a list, you have no idea whether he is literate or competent to judge your work, let alone possesses any clout with publishers. Even if he is all you'd like him to be, he will, as Yvonne has already observed in this book, take 15% of your profit, leaving you with next to nothing - even if your book is, by Canadian standards, at the lower end of the best seller range (some 5,000 or so copies sold).

My only attempt to find an agent was a disaster. This was many years ago. I thought that I should approach someone based in Ontario, where the majority of Canadian publishers are located, so I picked a name at random and sent my query off to his Toronto address. Weeks, then months, then years went by without a reply. Figuring that my letter had gone astray or that my would-be agent had fallen ill - maybe even died - I stopped expecting to hear and continued sending out my manuscripts on my own, a process I've never much liked doing because marketing a book takes considerable time away from one's writing and tends to dislodge one's mental notes about future works.

Anyway, to my utter amazement, two years after first attempting to contact him, I received a brief note from this agent informing me that he had just gotten around to opening his backlog of mail, but that, in any case, whatever my qualifications and potential, he was too busy to take me on.

Fortunately, by this time one of the books I had planned to send this man had been published in Ontario and was turning into a best seller for the small press there and another had been accepted by a Maritime press. I never have tried to find another agent.

A Typical Exchange:

By all means ring around the agents' offices.

Your call may go something like this:

Good morning. Walsh, Welfare and Washburn. How may I help you?

Uh, my name is Stephen King...

Gasp!

...sley.

Oh.

I have written a novel based on the life of Wilf Carter, and I would like to interest...

Oh, I'm sorry. Walsh, Welfare and Washburn are not able to take on new clients at present. Have a good day.

Wait! Perhaps if I spoke to Mr. Washburn...

Mr. Washburn is out of the country.

Mr. Walsh?

It's *Ms*, and she's busy.

But I...

Good-morning. So sorry we couldn't help you. Have a nice day.

Only if you can say:

"I'm Stephen King... Yes, *the* Stephen King, the writer..."

Only then will it turn out that Mr. Washburn is just returning from a week-end "down your way - Old Orchard Beach, heh-heh. Great little place! Great!" Or that Ms. Walsh just happens to be crossing the outer office at this very moment.

It's the old Catch 22 situation. When you need an agent, you can't interest one; when you don't need an agent... Be very clear. The agent you want - one who has an established business and a reputation for making good deals for clients; one who has the ear of influential publishers - that agent can't exist without money - lots of money - and is interested only in writers whose names are already household words, or whose books are likely to sell hundreds of thousands of copies.

Let's do the Math.

Your novel based on the life of Wilf Carter may sell 500 copies.

Oh, no!

'fraid so.

But I thought at least 50,000!

Let's get real here! 5000 copies constitutes a Canadian Best Seller... Listen. If your book sells for $20.00 - a high price today - that's $10,000, of which you, the author, may, if you're lucky, receive 10%, or $1000.

Hey! That's not fair!

Of course it isn't fair; it's business.

The distributor takes 40% (or more), you get 10% (or less) and the publisher keeps the rest to pay the bills with, and maybe has enough left over for a cup of coffee at Tim's. If the publisher offers you only 7.5%, don't be surprised.

You now have between $750 and $1000 to show for your several years' work and dedication, of which an agent would take 15%: something between 112.5 and 150 bucks. What was the total of *your* last month's phone bill?

No, Walsh, Welfare and Washburn will not be interested. They won't be interested in your manual on raising koalas in the basement either. How many Canadians will be? Maybe five? Add, say, 20 friends and relatives... (You may have many friends and relatives, but they'll all be waiting for their

free copy in their Christmas stocking - for which, by the way, you will pay
60% of list; authors receive 10 free copies of their works.)

Our advice? Forget agents. Save them for the long haul into the future.
The only ones you will reach now, while you're still unknown, will be strug-
gling for recognition as hard as you are, and probably won't have much
more in the way of contacts in the business.

As Allison says, some of them, too, won't know as much about writing as you do, and the partnership could be disastrous. I once approached
an agent - in Toronto - a very friendly, nice guy - who didn't know the
differences among "their," "there," and "they're." Our association didn't sur-
vive the argument over Their is a hole in there roof.

Small Publishers:

No, you don't need that kind of agent, but keep enquiring. It will be a
lot easier to negotiate from strength. That is, first find a *publisher* who will
speak directly to you. Then, if things go well, in a year or two you'll be able
to go back to Walsh, Welfare and Washburn as Stephen Kingsley, author of
that novel based on the life of Wilf Carter that did so well in Nashville.

ALLISON SAYS:

For some authors in some instances a small publishing house can be preferable to a large one. There are several reasons why this is so.

Big presses generally have big staffs and big overheads, so they need instant and sure-fire moneymakers, if they can find them. When one of their books first comes out there tends to be considerable media hype - as much fanfare as possible anyway - and, hopefully, good initial sales.

When sales start declining, the book is frequently remaindered - quickly. Warehousing the book is too costly. So after a brief flash in the pan the author may learn that his book is out of print - almost before he is accustomed to its being in print!

In contrast, astute editors and publishers of small publishing houses, with small staffs in close communication with one another, with fewer authors in their stables as well, and books they have usually thought long and hard about before taking them on, tend to keep many of their publications in stock for years, generally selling them more gradually than the big publishers, when they have a hit, but selling them steadily nonetheless. Although these small publishing houses may not have immediate best sellers, some of their publications may become best sellers in the long run.

Another advantage for the author dealing with a well run small press is that he or she can maintain personal contact with the editor and/ or publisher (sometimes one and the same). If a problem arises, it can be dealt with promptly and effectively because author, editor and publisher like and understand one another. In many large institutions, the close personal contacts are often shelved. The companies' chief decision-makers are at meetings (or extended coffee breaks) and the author finds himself pouring out his heart to an unresponsive voice mail instead of being able to discuss his concerns with a real person.

BITTER PILL TO SWALLOW:

What you have to offer a publisher;
> not the other way around.

Somebody once submitted a comprehensive
> sex manual to Harlequin!
Harlequin - at that time anyway - didn't even call
a spade a spade. (Though I was told, on good authority,
that they enjoyed the MS.)

Queries:

A small, local publishing house is your best bet. But remember: they all have their themes and you have to find out what you have to offer them before you make your pitch.

Find out each possible publisher's mandate. If the editors hold strictly to the rule "No Monkeys," don't bother them if you have been an organ grinder's assistant (even for a hundred years) and want to tell your story. "No Monkeys" can't help you.

Queries by Phone:

Once you have made a list of a few publishers you think might be interested in you and your work, proceed as follows:

Call on the phone.

Call from a place of peace and quiet - no screaming kids or noisy equipment.

Ask for the Acquisitions Editor - by name, if you can. If not, ask whoever answers the phone for the name.

Sound businesslike.

When you have reached the Acquisitions Editor,
Do *not* say:

I have a novel that's all ready for you.

Uh-uh. Publishers know very well that 99% of novels that come "all ready to publish" are no such thing.

Nor should you say:

I have a collection of short stories that will fit your list perfectly!

No, no. The editor is sure you know very little about the firm's lists - and she's probably right.

Never say:

Hi! I've got a book of poems that will make us millions!

(Exception: Say that if you want the publisher to die laughing.)

Books do, occasionally, make millions. Books of poetry usually don't clear expenses.

And publishers have all heard the millions story. Every time we hear it at DreamCatcher, we crack up. No matter how often we hear it, it's still funny.

Nor should you lose control of the conversation, like this:

Just after New Year's the phone rings at DreamCatcher...

You are calling from *Hawaii*?!

Yes.

Lucky you!

Yes.

Really? Hawaii? How's the weather out there?

Beautiful. I have this great story...

Oh. Then you must be a displaced Atlantic Canadian.

No. Actually I'm Australian.

Oh! How's the weather in good old Sydney?

I don't know. I haven't been back for over a year, but I have this great...

...story. Yes. What's your connection to Atlantic Canada?

Oh. Well...

I see.

But I know all about the west coast of Japan! I was there for three weeks. And I've written this great story about two Polynesians and a mako shark.

I picture our distributor's sales people rapidly going bald as they try to sell a book about two Polynesians and a mako shark to buyers who are expecting, maybe, advice on how to drive an oil tanker through right whale territory in thick Fundy fog.

I mean, think! Editors are busy people. Find one who already knows something about mako sharks. Then make your pitch.

Say Something Like:

Hi. Thanks for talking to me. How's your leg, by the way?
Sore in cold weather, thanks.
I'd like to send you the MS of my novel about two Polynesians and a mako shark, but if it's too painful...
No, it's good therapy for me. You're very thoughtful, though. Send your story along. I'll get to it. Give me six to eight weeks.

Queries by Post and e-mail:

Note: Remember that the name of your home town does not usually appear on an e-mail message. DreamCatcher's mandate - Atlantic Canadians first - requires that we know where you live. Others like to know too, for all kinds of reasons.

For instance:
I live in Truro, Nova Scotia.
Good. You're in.

I live in Bangor, Maine.
Well, you're outside our range - but not far - and probably you have friends or relatives on this side of the border, so we won't turn you down flat. But you'll have to be good.

I live in Brookline, Massachusetts.

No. Sorry. The only way we can consider your work is if you have written a terrific story based on global warming, climate change, planetary degradation... something "green."

Here are two Good beginnings:

Dear Ms. Wilson,

I was born in Sackville, New Brunswick and grew up there. I now live in Ontario, but my novel, which I hope you will read, is set on the Tantramar marshes.

Good. No problem. Both author and story connected.

Dear Ms. Wilson:

I have no connections of my own in Atlantic Canada, but my sister married a man from Prince Edward Island and I have been vacationing there every summer for the past six years.

OK, if you're very good. We'll take a look.

Next, we want to know what you have written and your theme.

Say I receive a letter that begins:
I live in Halifax, Nova Scotia.
Ok. You're eligible.

that goes on:
I have written a novel that I think is literary fiction...
Good...
...set in Los Angeles,
Oh, oh!
...about a boy who is a member of a gang

that deals drugs and comes into conflict with
the law...

No, you lost me. I was in Los Angeles once, thirty years ago, to visit Disney Land. I know nothing about gangs - anywhere - or dealing drugs, except what I see on TV. And though I may watch the occasional cop show, I click right on by shows about gangs. Also, I am not about to start researching gang warfare in LA, which is what I would have to do if I were to guide your story through the publishing process. You may have written the gang story of the century, *but* DreamCatcher won't be interested. Gangs/drugs is not one of our themes, and you are away out of our geographic range.

We suspect, too, that you probably expect your story to become a film. Again we can't help you. We have no agents or contacts who could take your story through the steps. On that road, agents have to have agents - to have agents!

If we saw your story as potentially the greatest film of the century - another *West Side Story*, for example - we might try to give you a boost toward an agent. But if we saw it as just one of a series, such as we can find on TV any night of the week, we wouldn't be interested.

No, if you're going to write about LA, you need an agent there. We work out of a small city on Canada's east coast. To interest DreamCatcher, a story has to have our kind of flavour - something special and (usually) down-east - that sets it off from the hundreds of thousands of others that appear:

- an important theme that interests us
- an engrossing character
- an intriguing presentation
- a moving atmosphere.

ALLISON SAYS:

The regional structure of this country has always played a significant role in Canadian literature and is an important consideration in finding a publisher. By and large, readers at the west coast, on the prairies, in Ontario and Quebec are not, first and foremost, interested in books set in the Maritimes. Similarly, Maritimers generally prefer to read about their own part of the country. The one region which seems to intrigue readers from all across Canada - though Maritimers less than others - is the North.

A Maritime book generally needs a Maritime publisher, though there have been notable exceptions to this rule - novelists such as New Brunswicker, David Adams Richards, who has published his much acclaimed and prize-winning Miramichi novels in Toronto, and Antonine Maillet, another New Brunswicker who has published many of her now internationally famous books on 'Acadie' (such as La Sagouine) in Montreal. However, it is worth noting that Richards moved to Toronto several years ago to be near his publisher, and Maillet spends part of most years in Montreal.

All the books I have written which are set in the Maritimes have had Maritime publishers, and by and large these books have done well in this region - and some of them, eventually, in other parts of the country.

Where I have run into some initial difficulties has been with several books set in western Canada. With two of these I made inquiries of three western Canadian presses and was turned down before I could present them with a manuscript because of my long-time residency in the Maritimes. One press even returned my letter unopened because the editor assumed, he wrote, that with an address in Atlantic Canada, I would have nothing to say that would interest his company. He underlined the fact that his press published only books by contemporary residents of his province. That a writer might once have lived in his province for some time, and that the contemporary resident might only recently have moved there did not apparently enter into his calculations.

If you have written a book about the North or the aboriginal people you generally need to look for a publisher whose chief focus is on these subjects. For The Northern Imagination and my Grey Owl books, as well as several articles and poems *with northern themes, I was fortunate in finding such a publisher - in Ontario - and these publications did well.*

However, two other books with northern themes, Taku and Atlin, the last utopia were published by my long-time Nova Scotia publisher, and were also successful. Taku won two prestigious prizes in British Columbia and Atlin went through three printings.

BITTER PILL:

In short, the MS that excites DreamCatcher is about something familiar to us that has some connection, however tenuous, to the North Atlantic Shore.

(I speak of DreamCatcher, but what I say applies to most publishers.)

Copyright:

Inexperienced writers often think that publishers simply take lucky MSS and have them printed - but that, while *we* are at it, *they* had better register copyright or *we*'ll rob *them* blind.

The truth is
- that the copyright is yours.
- that publishers have far more - far, far more - submissions than they can ever deal with, and most of them (face it!) will be better than yours - at least for the publisher's needs.
- that publishers have far more to do than to print (or reprint) books, without telling the authors, so that they can keep the profits.

Mirielle's novel didn't sell - many don't. But it was a nice little story and the publisher kept a few copies in the office.

One afternoon a pleasant, middle-aged lady dropped in and asked for Mirielle's title. The publisher sold it to her. Boys, oh boys! as we say in the Maritimes, the next morning Mirielle arrived smoking mad. The publisher was selling *her* books and keeping *her* royalties.

Mirielle had sent a spy. Instead of simply asking; instead of learning a bit about how the business was run, Mirielle stayed home till she had stewed herself to boiling point; then she made herself look foolish.

CHAPTER TWO:

YOUR ACQUISITIONS EDITOR

**Here's how a TYPICAL DAY begins in the life of a
small publisher's ACQUISITIONS EDITOR.**

I arrive in the office at eleven.

Elizabeth says, "There's another MS for you. I put it on your desk."

Chas says, "You've got X number of e-mail queries. I printed them out for you. One of them attached the whole MS - 280 pages. I didn't print that, of course, but if you want to see it..."

"No. Most unlikely."

I sit down and look at the package that contains the MS. I am checking for the name of the sender and the return address.

"H'mm. Chamberlaine, Ontario. I don't remember agreeing to read anything from there."

I check my list. No, never heard of this one. But I have five minutes...
I open the package. Look for a covering letter. Find one.

Maybe the letter begins

> Dear Dream Catcher:
>> *Might have got the goofy spelling right!*
>
> Or - This is a winner! To whom it may concern:
>> *Don't concern me, honey. I'm not the least bit concerned.*
>
> Sometimes letters are addressed simply, Dear Editor.
>> *Well-l-l...*
>
> Or Dear Mrs. Margaris:
>> *No, no. Mrs. Margaris is the publisher.*
>> *You want the Acquisitions Editor, who happens to be me.*
>
> Ah! Dear Ms. Wilson:
>> *Knows my name at least...*

But then - and I'm not kidding - the letter may say something like this:

> Dear Ms. Wilson:
>
> I am sending you the MS of my work-in-progress, a novel called *Men from Mars*, because I need to know if you will publish it when it is finished. I don't want to go to all the trouble of writing it if it isn't going to be published.
>
> Any suggestions you can make will be gratefully received.
>
> Yours truly,
> John

I wrote that letter myself, but I have received many like it.

John, (I would like to reply...)

Dear John,

Just outside my window, just beyond the door to this building, just a moment's walk from my desk lies Saint John Harbour, which leads to the Bay of Fundy, which leads to the North Atlantic Ocean. The ocean is full of hungry fish, and porpoises, and (in the summertime) whales. I don't know whether or not these life forms like inky paper, but on my way home I will drop your pages into the water...

I would like to reply like that, but I don't. Nor do I ever shout at the top of my lungs:

No, John, I will NOT read your MS and tell you if we will publish it when it is finished, because

100:1	You won't finish it.
1000:1	It won't be ready to publish if you do.
10000:1	DreamCatcher won't be interested - if and when.

No. I am a nice person. I don't do that. Instead I sing a few bars of

> *"No, no, a thousand times no.*
> *I'd rather die than say yes."*

(Bar-room ditty of the late 19th.c.)

Then I write:

Dear John,

DreamCatcher likes to see finished MSS when assessing the work of young writers we don't know. Finish your story as well as you can, and try again.

Even Elizabeth (Mrs. Margaris) who will give anybody a hearing, says, "I can't do a thing till I see a finished manuscript."

DO YOUR RESEARCH

I mentioned this before:

LIBRARIES HAVE REFERENCES THAT LIST HUNDREDS OF PUBLISHERS, NAME THEIR ACQUISITIONS EDITORS, AND EXPLAIN THE KINDS OF MSS THEY READ.

Study appropriate references.
Sift through them.
Don't blanket the world with queries; hone in
on promising places.
And always confess to multiple queries.

BITTER PILL:

Many publishers won't reply to multiple queries. Unless your name is John Grisham or Danielle Steele, they're not interested in competing for your work and can't put their time and effort into reading what you send. Don't expect a reply. But do expect their displeasure if you don't say this is a multiple and get caught. On the off-chance that you had two fish on your hook, you would be liable to lose both.

ALLISON SAYS:

Most publishing houses request the author to query before submitting a manuscript. Presses should answer these queries within a reasonable time. Also, once the manuscript is in the editor's hands, the author should expect to have his or her manuscript accepted or rejected within a stipulated time. Reply within three months is often the rule - though not necessarily.

A disheartening number of editors/publishers (of both books and magazines) do not get back to the author within an acceptable time. Like most writers, I have had several bad experiences.

One well-known Ontario publishing house kept a book manuscript the editor had agreed to consider for months, which ran into years. When, after two years had elapsed, I wrote to ask what was what, the editor said she was sorry but she didn't know what had happened - that "they" seemed to have lost my manuscript.

In another instance, a small press in western Canada kept a manuscript for two years, and, in a rejection letter, said that "they" had been interested, but had decided that they couldn't afford to publish any more books in the immediate future. Not only had they taken all that time to come to such a conclusion, but with the rejection letter they sent me someone else's manuscript - a sheaf of poems, not my novel!

It's because of incidents like this that some authors make multiple submissions. So although I agree with Yvonne that for an editor - especially such a thoughtful and diligent one as she is - multiple submissions are terrible (an editor having invested considerable time and thought in a manuscript, only to find that another publishing house has already glommed onto it), the author who has been left dangling by disorganized/uncaring editors and publishers is also in a dreadful position.

So although I have not myself made multiple submissions, I can see why some authors do - though if they do, they need to warn the editor to whom they have sent their work that he or she is in competition for the manuscript.

In Reply to Queries:

Because DreamCatcher is a small house, and because I'm a writer myself and know how hard it is to be heard by the publishing business, I nearly always send a short hand-written note in reply to queries. And I often receive back something like this:

Dear Yvonne,

Thank-you for answering my query. I sent out 150 letters and got 6 replies. Of the 6, yours was the only one that wasn't just a printed rejection form. I really appreciated hearing from a real person. Good luck to DreamCatcher.

Frustrated Author

By the Way: Always send SASE. (self-addressed stamped envelopes) for reply or return of MS.

Note: Letters *must* bear the stamp of the country of origin. That is, if I mail you a letter in Saint John, it has to have a Canadian stamp. I don't know how many SASE I have received from American writers that had US stamps affixed. If you're crossing borders, remember: Most post offices can supply international postal vouchers - sort of little money orders. The publisher just has to present one of these at a Post Office and stamps appear in exchange.

Now here's a GOOD query letter:

Dear Ms. Wilson:

I have heard from the Writer's Federation of New Brunswick that DreamCatcher is reading MSS of novels with "green" themes.

I spend my summers scuba diving in the Bay of Fundy and the southern Gulf and the rest of the year working toward my first degree in English Literature at Mount A.

These two activities have led to my first novel, that I call *Rising Water*, about a young man, like myself, who feels driven to give up plans to become a well-paid accountant in his parents' firm to study marine biology instead. This decision leads to conflict with the young man's family and his girlfriend, but in the end his parents are convinced that his life will be useful and rewarding, if not very successful in terms of money and recognition, and he finds a new love when he meets a girl in his biology lab who has the same interests.

The novel is as good as I can make it on my own. My friends like it, and one of my professors has said, "It is quite good, and I think you should send it to a publisher." I therefore hope you will read it. I am not approaching any other publisher at this time.

Very truly yours,

Omnipotus P. Quinibus.

P.S. Do you think I should use a pseudonym?

Points to Ponder:

1. Omni has written to *me*: Dear Ms. Wilson. That's good.

2. Omni begins by explaining how he knows about DreamCatcher. Very good. Places both of us on firm ground.

3. Omni wastes no words but goes straight on to introduce himself and his novel *Rising Water*.

4. Omni briefly (Excellent) describes the theme of his novel and gives a one-sentence outline of the plot.

5. He confesses that he has done his best. He is not overconfident, or over diffident. He says his friends like his novel (but friends always do.) And he gives his professor's exact words, even though they do not explode with praise.

6. He signs his name and asks for my opinion.

My answer to his question: Call yourself Omni Quinibus. That will be enough. ***Do not use a pseudonym.*** Your publisher will expect you to help publicize the book, and you don't want people whispering, "I thought that guy was Omni Quin-something!" when you are introduced as Brad Abs.

My thoughts on reading this letter?
Good. Author meets DC's criteria
     knows my name
     has finished his MS but asks me to "read" it, not
     "publish" it
On the other hand:
     he's pretty young and inexperienced
     we'd probably have to do a rewrite
     but, yes. I'll take a look.

BITTER PILL:

Publishers are wary of very young authors because they are often

- arrogant
- superior to the world in general and old editors in particular
- sure they're going to be rich and famous overnight – and it's the publisher's fault when they're not!

What Most Publishers are looking for:
A big name (the author's)
Non-fiction (especially self-help and spiritual)
A title that will sell millions of copies.

Note: Not many publishers do fiction nowadays. Or put another way, most publishers (publishing is a business after all) prefer to do non-fiction because non-fiction sells; fiction doesn't.

But a lot of dreams went "pop" when Oprah gave up her book club, and they weren't only authors' dreams.

Then what do publishers take? Because there's a lot of stuff in the stores, and...

Well, I'd say it's a cross between what they like and what they think they can sell.

Editors have personal tastes and lots to choose from.

For example, *I* think - it's a personal opinion or taste - that portraying certain sections of this country as backward, poverty stricken, cold and bleak, and the people as depraved, amoral, and sub-normal constitutes a slander, and I won't acquire MSS like that for my publisher. She indulges me. We both know that these stories have been selling well and making fine reputations for years. But I have to read and reread books we publish. I have to work on them for a year or two - maybe more - till they are as good as I think the authors can make them. By that time I, and the authors, have pretty well memorized them. I'm not going to choose something that depresses me and makes me sick, especially if I think it's an unfair depiction of an area and its people.

BITTER PILL:

Unless you hit upon a formula that the world is hungry for, your fiction won't make money, for you or for your publisher.

But never mind, there is always somebody publishing fiction for the love of it. Fiction writers just have to look harder and keep at it longer. And be ready to promote, promote, promote yourself.

Perhaps you will think, when you read about Allison's experiences as a book editor, that there is very little similarity between my work and hers. But this dissimilarity is only in the details; in the types of projects we undertake. Our work is similar, even identical, in premise:

We are entrusted with the creations of others, to prepare them for publication, and we owe to both the work and the author the greatest respect and courtesy.

It is the function of the editor to bring out the best qualities in both work and author; to see that both author and work appear in clear, strong light; that the work as a whole is unified; and that the effect on the reader is as close as possible to the author's intent.

ALLISON SAYS:

My Stints as Editor

More Labor-Intensive Efforts
Than I Would Have Thought

edit: "set in order for publication (material chiefly provided by others)."
editor: "one who prepares the work of others for publication."
- Oxford Dictionary

I never expected to be an editor - never set out to work for a publishing house - and when I did find myself cast in this role it was not in a full-time or long-term position. Consequently, my experiences as editor have been different from those of my friend Yvonne Wilson, in-house editor at DreamCatcher Publishing.

Nevertheless, to my surprise really, I have in the past ten years been editor of three books and co-editor of two others. Truly, life is full of unexpected occurrences!

Three of these five books were other people's ideas. For these three I was asked to be an editor. The first book I edited was in this category - that is, it was not my idea.

In 1992 my then long-term Nova Scotia publisher, Bill Pope of Lancelot Press, had just accepted Taku when he asked me if, as my next literary project, I would select and introduce a collection of Alden Nowlan's poetry and prose. He thought the time was right for publishing such a book. He had already chosen the title - The Best of Alden Nowlan.

I agreed promptly to this request: first of all because I had always liked Alden Nowlan's work, particularly his poetry; and secondly because I felt indebted to Bill for accepting Taku - a book set in northern British Columbia, the Yukon and Alaska

- which, I worried, might not find a sufficient Maritime readership.

As it happened, both *Taku* and *The Best of Alden Nowlan* came out in 1993, both did well and both received very good reviews.

What had surprised me, however, when working on the Nowlan book, was that editing this collection was such a lot of work. It turned out in fact to be what old-timers would have called a tall order.

First of all it entailed reading all of Nowlan's books anew. After all, I reckoned, how can you choose the pieces you think are best without reading everything you can lay your hands on shortly before making your selections?

As I read and read - and reread - I told myself repeatedly that it was just as well that I liked Nowlan's writing so much. I was fortunate not only in that regard, but also because I had the Mount Allison University Library with its good collection of Nowlan's works close at hand, as well as access through inter-library loan to other volumes not in the library.

Even so, the research took a lot of time and thought - certainly more than I had expected. Although this undertaking had not been such a monumental task as researching and writing Taku, nevertheless a great deal of effort was involved. Indeed, working on this book was when I learned just how labor-intensive this kind of editing can be.

Despite this realization, I was soon (before the year was out) engaged in another demanding editorial project.... Choosing pieces for the Nowlan collection and writing what I hoped was a persuasive introduction to it had turned my thoughts to bringing together in a similar format the prose and poetry of another writer, Alice Cameron Brown - my mother.

She had died in January 1993, leaving me, her literary executor, with bundles of unsorted papers. These included published stories and poems (or references to them), sheaves of typed or hand-written manuscripts and letters from such significant luminaries of Canadian Literature as B.K. Sandwell and Earle Birney, perhaps her most appreciative and encouraging mentors.

Her correspondence and the lists of writers who flanked her magazine and anthology publications reads like a Who's Who of Canadian editors, writers and literary agents of the years in which she appeared most frequently on the Canadian literary scene (the thirties and forties).

Eventually I found pieces I especially liked in Saturday Night (when B.K. Sandwell was editor), The Canadian Poetry Magazine (when E.J. Pratt and, later, Earle Birney were editors), The Canadian Author and Bookman, Mayfair, Chatelaine, The Globe and Mail, the Writers Studio Fiction (1936) - a prize-winning piece, and in such hardcover anthologies as New Canadian Anthology (Crucible Press, 1938). Several children's poems, written in the thirties, appeared later, in Gage's prize-winning book, The Nunny Bag (1962).

Among my difficulties in making up this collection was finding her published pieces. (Mostly she hadn't kept copies, though there were references to some of them in letters). Eventually, I tracked down enough for a small collection. This came out in 1993 (the same year as Taku and the Nowlan book.)

Another matter which held me up when I had almost finished selecting and arranging my mother's pieces was finding a suitable cover. Because at the beginning of her writing career, during the Depression, she had won an award and accolades, both in the West and Ontario, for her poem "Burning Straw Stacks", I wanted to call the collection after this poem and choose a cover picture which would do justice to this fiery and extraordinary phenomenon.

After writing archives and libraries near and far, it became apparent that such a picture did not exist, or, if it did, I couldn't unearth it. Since I still had my sights firmly set on such a cover, I decided to ask for my daughter Naomi's help in recreating in watercolors a scene I remembered from my early childhood - another tall order. From my description she came up with a beautiful cover, depicting burning straw stacks against a night sky as I remembered them.

The bringing together in this instance of words and a pictorial illustration once more underlines the assertion I have made elsewhere in this book of the importance for me, in certain circumstances, of the connection between these two art forms.

My third attempt at editing, The Best of Abraham Gesner, was an easier undertaking than the two preceding ones because, by the time I was ready to put this collection together, I already had all the material I wanted close at hand. I had selected the pieces I needed - along with suitable illustrations - while working on a Gesner biography, Prophet of the Wilderness, convinced that many of Gesner's writings needed rescuing from the obscurity of long out-of-print publications. Both my Gesner books were published in 1995.

The last two books I was involved in editing were *Poetic Voices of the Maritimes, a Selection of Contemporary Poetry* (1996) and *Maritime Voices, Twentieth Century Stories by Women* (2000). Both books were suggested by my friend and former student, Dr. Theresia Quigley. Jointly we chose selections and edited these books.

Although I can imagine that co-editing such books could be a problem under certain circumstances, Professor Quigley and I had no difficulties. We worked very well together. In both instances she and I each chose roughly half the authors and wrote the introductory pieces on their work. Throughout these undertakings we compared notes. Both books have been well received.

BITTER PILL:

The publisher has the last word. DreamCatcher always tries to work with the author - most publishers try to do that - but if they come to impasse, the publisher decides on the final text, the publisher decides the format, paper weight, cover art, number of copies to be printed, and so on.

Remember:

Good editors never make changes to the MSS of living authors, or to any of the works of those who are no longer with us, except, when working with very old MSS or publications, to update punctuation.

Editors make suggestions. We say, "No, no. This punctuation isn't doing what you want it to do." Or, "I don't think you mean to say what you actually say here." Or, "I would delete this page." Then we leave you to decide and to make appropriate changes.

For a year or two I worked with Webster, till it became clear to me that he was not going to learn the craft. He had an unbridled imagination and could spend long hours at his computer without tiring or running out of ideas. But he had no grasp of how to... He didn't even recognize a sentence when he saw one. I had to cast him aside. He expected me to do his work for him.

Even when the editing of your MS has progressed to the final stages before printing, a good editor will still require *you* to make necessary changes. Her notes may have shortened to simple directives: delete... tighten... punc (punctuate) but the implication will still be there: this is your work; you do it. It is only if a writer is hell bent (in my opinion) on ruining a MS by refusing to consider a requested change, that I draw the line. It is only then that I put my foot down and say, "No. Here I stand. I won't take the blame for your folly."

Mary Lou insisted on a passage that I felt ruined the flow of her narrative. From day one I advised against that passage, but every time the problem came up, she had a reason for keeping it. Eventually I had to say, "No, Mary Lou. Here I stand in battle armour."

What would be the outcome if we came to Mexican stand-off? Well, Mary Lou would say, "No. It's my book. I want it my way." I would then shrug and take the problem to my publisher, who would say, "Mary Lou, sweetie, are you raising the several thousand dollars we need to pay the printer for this book? No? Well then, you have a choice: either you accept the advice of my editorial staff, or there will be no book." We have never come to that. But...

No editor wants to fight with writers. We'll try every persuasion. We believe in diplomacy and discussion. But... The problem is, kids, that it's the editor who gets the blame for your mistakes. She's not just being cantankerous; she has her own reputation to lose. Listen to her/him. Your editor is your best friend, mentor, adviser, father, mother, and sainted aunt. Listen to him/her.

Acceptance:

And then you wait.

By this time you've read so much about how hard it is to break into print; you've heard so much from publishers, agents, editors, and other writers, that you begin to wonder: Is it true? Is there really a book publishing industry after all? Or is this just another scam, just another Tooth Fairy scenario?

Yes, Virginia, there really is a book publishing industry. When doubts assail, go to a large book store or library and look around. But don't stay too long; you may begin to shrink, like Alice, under the sheer total of the volumes on the shelves. Stay long enough to convince yourself that you are not fantasizing the whole thing; then rush home to work. Because...

If you work smart

If you keep learning

If you never give up

If you're a complete masochist...

One of these days the phone will ring or there will be a letter in your box...

Dear Virginia,

Please send the MS of your novel *Yellow Sunbury Trucks* for reading by our editors.

Allow 6 to 8 weeks, or 3 months, or...

Now rush outside and holler your head off. Don't do it in the house. Not only will you scare the family if you do; you may be in danger of fracturing your cranium on the ceiling.

Format:

The letter will probably tell you how to present your MS. That is: hard copy, disk, etc. *Read this part carefully and follow it* **TO THE LETTER.**

Most book publishers still ask for hard copy (one side only) on 8.5" x 11" white, non-correctable paper (that means you can't erase mistakes; therefore, ink won't rub off all over hands and other pages.)

They'll want your work double-spaced, and they'll want 1" - 1.5" margins. They may not state font size, but remember, the occupational hazard of the editing fraternity is eye strain; print large enough for comfortable reading: 12 point is good.

Be sure you use headers on every page; I like the top line *on every page* to read:

Your Name	Name of MS	Page #
as		
Merryweather	The Terrible Storm	1

We receive all kinds of patterns, but I find having the page number in the upper right-hand corner facilitates my work. And you do want to keep your editor in a good mood!

Punctuation is important. At this point, neatness counts - a lot. But *do not* decorate your pages (even your title page) and do not bind your pages.

I know that sending off a MS without some kind of cover or clip feels like sending your kids to school without shoes, but do it. The first thing the editor will do with your binder is to rip it off - maybe with a snarl. And art work on the title page looks unprofessional.

Title pages should show in the upper left-hand corner:

> Your full name
> Mailing address
> Phone numbers
> E-mail addresses
> WebSite addresses

In the upper right-hand corner:

> Number of words
> Number of pages

In the middle of the page

Title	The Terrible Storm
by	by
You	Terrence Merryweather

These requirements may seem arbitrary, but there are good reasons for all of them. Editors want double-spacing and unbound hard copy because they want to be able to make notes on the MS, and some of their notes will spill over onto the back of the page. And we want hard copy as opposed to disks because we will almost certainly want to suggest changes, and that won't work electronically: A good book editor will not make changes without the author's agreement.

Note: Editors speak of authors they work with as *their* writers, as doctors speak of *their* patients and teachers of *their* students. The relationship is close, mutually supportive, and should be professional.

Finally, package your MS in a strong envelope - ordinary manila covers often arrive in bad shape - enclose:

a covering letter

a stamped postcard if you want confirmation of receipt

and an SASE for return of the MS, if you want it back.

Do NOT send the disk - not yet.

Do NOT send original illustrations or photographs.

Do NOT send designs for the book cover.

> I have said that I like to meet authors who are about forty. At that age they have found out they're not the hottest thing to hit town since the fire that destroyed the dinosaurs, but they do not yet feel old age rushing upon them.

Exceptions to this rule:

Kali Brazier-Tompkins, whose first novel came out when she was sixteen, who has always been a joy to work with.

Muriel Mackenzie, who was ninety-two when DreamCatcher published her picture book "The Crooked Little Tree." A delightful client.

And we have writers well spread out between these two.

Celebrate:

You've reached an important milestone. A publisher has consented to read your MS.

Celebrate.

Don't wait till you have your book between covers in your hand. Celebrate each step along the way.

Thank your first readers for their encouragement, and ask them to keep it up - away from potential publishers, of course.

Explain to your parents that finding the "just right" publisher for your book is progressing nicely but may take time. Their buttons will be in even greater danger of busting off if they think you are going to be careful in your choice. Not just any old publisher will do for their kid, after all! They're not to know that you and your great opus are now at the mercy of the cold and cruel world as manifested in the person of an Acquisitions Editor who may flay the skin off this child of your heart before flinging it back REJECTED!

BITTER PILL:

Try to find an editor who is also a writer. Most of them will let you down as painlessly as they can. Most, but not all!

Rejection:

Make your spouse understand that the car will have to do a while longer.

And convince the children - if you can - that they will enjoy Disney World much more in a year or two when they have grown a little bigger.

Then convince yourself that your dreams of instant recognition and overnight success need to be pruned back. This step may be the hardest of all. But try as hard as you can to take it; you will be much happier if you can.

Because...

the truth is...

when you have thought of every reason under the sun for rejection, publishers will come up with one that they dragged out from under the moon.

Ceci sent us a story for kids about magic, runes, mysterious evils... It came straight from her mind and heart and was, she was sure, the most original thing this century. Only, somebody else - a big name writer - all unbeknownst to Ceci - had already written her story. (Ceci had missed it growing up, but there it was.)

Beat that for an unexpected reason for rejection!

Note: When you are writing, you may sometimes think, "Have I read this somewhere?" There's more about originality elsewhere in this book.

Poppy asked us to read a collection of short stories. I did. And they weren't stories. I'm not sure what they were.

Lex submitted a novel that had won a provincial contest. George had been assisted by a Canada Council grant to write his book. I found that both MSS needed much work before they would be ready for publication. But neither Lex nor George would believe me. Had Lex not won a prize? Had George not been subsidized by the Canada Council? They must, therefore, be first class.

Suzie won a contest. I read her story. It wasn't bad, though it could have been greatly improved. But it had won first prize! It was, therefore, never improved.

BITTER PILL:

Is it possible - just possible - that your story that won the contest was the best of a *mediocre* lot?

In my opinion, among the most damaging events in a young writer's life are winning a contest and receiving a grant.

Note: Young writers are beginners. Age has nothing to do with it.

Never rest on your laurels.

Laurels scratch something cruel if you sit on them.

Don't Be Devastated by the Thought of Rejection:

> **Remember,**
> **Writing is Art.**
> **Publishing is business.**
> **Rejection doesn't mean that your work is bad, necessarily.**

Victor sent us a beautiful novel. It was well written, well designed, well balanced, beautifully conceived and presented, and tied up in red ribbon. But we couldn't take it. It was so erudite, so high brow, so (we judged) narrow in its appeal, we couldn't see selling more than a couple of hundred copies. And coming off the Chapters losses and then the General Distributing bankruptcy, we couldn't take the chance. I would have given next year's Diet Coke to publish that book, but we couldn't do it.

Victor had submitted his MS to one of the big houses before he came to us. They didn't tell him why they decided, in the end, not to publish him, but I suspect their reason was the same as ours - they just couldn't see clearing their expenses.

If you come to DreamCatcher and we turn you down, I'll tell you why. Bigger publishers may not tell you, but their reasons also range widely and may have nothing to do with quality.

Never take rejection as the end of your career as a writer.

- Keep writing.
- Keep learning.
- Stay humble enough to see huge possibilities for improvement - in time.
- Keep sending out queries.
- Submit your MS to any publisher who will read it, one at a time.
- Remember that nobody is going to steal it. Even if someone were tempted - most unlikely! - nothing would happen. Your work is not that good - yet. And the copyright is yours.
- Start on your next book.
- Start right away enquiring from publishers whether they might be interested in your next book when it's ready.

Note: This kind of query is not the same as the one on p. 24 in which the writer wants the publisher to read an unfinished MS. This kind asks if the publisher is interested in your theme and gives a date when you hope to have the MS ready for reading:

Dear Ms. Wilson:

I am writing a novel set in Halifax on the theme of loss of habitat for shore birds. The protagonist is a PhD student at St. Mary's who becomes interested in the subject through an elderly lady in a wheelchair who watches birds from her tenth floor window.

I hope to have the MS ready for reading by June of next year. I would be pleased if you would consider it for publication.

Yours very truly,

This query is just making a head start, and is not at all likely to make me sing my bar-room song.

- And short of being a nuisance, keep in touch with

> Val came in with a novel I enjoyed because the theme was one of my special favourites, but it was not a story that DreamCatcher was looking for at the time. I would have enjoyed working on it, but...
>
> I was in the middle of explaining to Val why we couldn't accept his MS, when he said, "I have another - the second one I wrote - that may be closer to what you want." It was.

What am I telling you?
Many things. But perhaps in a nutshell I am saying:

- ❖ If you write a novel, you are a novelist.
- ❖ If you write poems, you are a poet.
- ❖ If you write journal articles, you are a journalist.

And it doesn't make one iota of difference whether you are published or not.

❖ If you write because that is what you do with your ideas, you are a writer.
❖ If you enjoy the process of writing, you are a writer.
❖ If time disappears when you are writing and you suddenly realize it's two o'clock in the morning and you haven't eaten yet, you're a writer.
❖ If writing makes you happy, never give it up; it's what you're for.

Note: A few years ago, Ray Bradbury, one of my favourite writers, wrote a little book called *Zen in the Art of Writing*. (Highly recommended.)

ALLISON SAYS:

Large numbers of people say they plan to write a book - and will put pen to paper just as soon as time and circumstances permit. I've heard all kinds of people make this claim - a claim supported by the widely circulated view that nearly everyone is harboring at least one book (one story anyway) which is worth telling.

Although I believe that almost everyone does indeed have the makings of a book, what I know is that actually getting the words down in readable form is not as quick and easy as a lot of people

*imagine. Besides, an entire book for most begin-
ning writers is a tall order. Starting with a short
story, essay or poems makes more sense and seems
manageable because of a much shorter time frame.
Then, if one of these shorter pieces works out, tack-
ling a book perhaps won't seem so daunting.*

*At least this has been my experience. When my
children were young and later when I was working at a demanding job, completing my doctor-
ate and raising a family, I knew that the books I
dreamed of writing would have to wait quite some
time to see the light. Consequently, I began with a
lot of poems, a children's story and scads of articles. When these were published promptly and were
well received I was encouraged to believe that as
soon as I had a breathing spell I would tackle a
book.*

**You now have an idea of what book editors do, how they think
and feel and how they approach their work.**

**In particular, we hope you have a better idea than you had be-
fore we began of why acquisitions editors may not be enthusiastic
about your third (all unpublished) novel, called *The Life of Laura
Lindsay: my Great-Great Grandmother* (1852-1876). Nothing personal.
It's just that they are already up to their ears in terrific projects.**

CHAPTER THREE:

My manuscript is being read.

    What Happens No-o-o-ow?

Well, don't start biting your nails.

Don't take to drink.

My advice is: start writing your next book.

The result may not be the fame and riches you dream of, but

- it won't do any harm
- you'll have a lot of fun doing it
- and if your first effort is rejected, you won't mind so much, because you will have half-forgotten it already. (The book you're working on is always the best. And so it should be if you keep on learning.)

Remember:

Your publisher IS NOT your enemy.

Your editor IS your friend and advocate.

YOU ARE NOW ONE OF A TEAM.

Note: *One* of a *Team.*

- Never show your editor "attitude."
- Never let your publisher hear you whine.
- Short of being a nuisance, keep in touch with the publisher. If possible, drop in from time to time. Take the editor out for a Coke and a half hour's conversation once in a while. If you are not near, cards and e-mail messages are good. Phone calls are not so good; they often interrupt the editor's train of thought. But if we never hear from you, you'll be pushed to the edge of the desk and passed over till the day you fall off and scatter all over the floor.

ABOVE ALL, BE PATIENT.

WHILE YOU WAIT:

You won't be alone while you wait the 6 to 8 or more weeks your busy editor has asked for. Look around. Nearly everybody is waiting for something. How many strawberry growers do you know? Listen to them in early summer: "If it doesn't rain today or tomorrow..." "If we have a couple of days of sun..." "If I can find help to pick the crop..."

Or perhaps you hunt ducks. I object to hunting, and duck hunters would object to me if they knew I was awake early on the first of October, willing the birds to escape. I am happy when the guns stop on the second or third because the ducks have all disappeared. But cold and wet, the hunters sit in the blinds, then gather at the Irving to drink hot coffee and mutter to anyone who will listen: "Not like when I was a kid. The sky was black with them then. Well, maybe next year. The water is too high this fall (or too low.) Maybe next year."

I used to know a very good badminton player. Usually he won. But if he didn't, his racquet always needed restringing, or its frame needed straightening.

Don't be like that fellow. Grow strawberries. I'd even rather you hunted ducks. Accept responsibility for your work and keep on learning. Your brain doesn't need restringing; you need to learn how to write what you have to say. Your frame doesn't need straightening; you need to realize that writing is a craft as well as an art form, and you have to learn the craft.

Would you set out to make a suit of formal clothes without knowing the basics of tailoring? Of course you wouldn't. You wouldn't even set out to make a nightshirt for the baby without knowing how to use needle and thread. You'd know you would be setting yourself up for failure. Yet well over half of the aspiring writers who bring their MSS to DreamCatcher have worked, sometimes for years, without the slightest acquaintance with themes, narrators, points of view, how to present a character, how to make a point... So many make the same mistakes that I sometimes gather a bunch together and give a week-end seminar just so I won't have to teach them the same lessons one at a time.

So maybe you should take a course or attend a seminar on writing while you wait.

As Allison Says:

WRITING CLASSES

Writing classes and seminars are not for everyone. They are only one way to get started, to encourage oneself by writing regularly and getting some prompt feedback - feedback one rarely gets from sending off one's early efforts to a publisher.

If one is interested in trying out his or her potential as a poet, short story writer, novelist or writer of creative non-fiction, it is important that the person giving the course or seminar has had considerable experience and some success in these genres. Otherwise, the dialogues and judgements in and out of class are not necessarily useful.

These days most North American universities give credit courses in creative writing at the undergraduate level - and some at the graduate level. As well, they often sponsor non-credit seminars and courses, besides hiring established writers-in-residence for short-term positions. These established writers, while carrying on with their own work, are available at limited times for consultation with aspiring writers.

Under auspicious circumstances, a writing class can provide the would-be writer with important insights into his or her creative capabilities - or lack of these talents. Either way, finding out is worthwhile.

What is also significant is that such a class can be taken at any age. It is possible to discover one's writing talents and hone them in middle or old age when undertaking and excelling in other new careers - competitive sports or medicine, for instance - are no longer possible.

A startling instance of an elderly would-be writer who found herself through a creative writing course is Harriet Doerr. At age 65, because of a dare from her son, she returned to college, enrolled in creative writing courses and subsequently, in her seventies and eighties, turned out three remarkable and acclaimed books. The first of these, a novel Stones for Ibarra (1984), won the American Book Award. Another novel, Consider This, Señora, and a collection of essays, The Tiger in the Grass, were also successful.

By and large, most of the successful aspiring writers in my courses, as far as I know, have been, to some extent at least, inspired by literary models which intrigued them - poems, stories, novels which they enjoyed reading and discussing and to which they responded with their own creations.

For instance, in an introductory poetry class, one of the students, an eighteen year old, wrote several ballads for an in-class presentation. Since down through the ages ballads have traditionally been sung, this young man, an accomplished fiddler, set his words to music and sang them.

His ballads were original and touching, and, with their musical accompaniment, just right. The class applauded enthusiastically. Some years later this young man became well known for the music and lyrics he wrote and staged.

Another member of this same class began writing poetry at this time, but did not hand in any of her poems for class assignments, producing instead conventional essays. She said at the time that she was not yet ready to let anyone read her poems.

At various times over the years, when we ran into one another, shopping and at a restaurant, she told me she was still writing and still not sending out her poems for publication. Then, just a few years ago, I read in a newspaper that she had won first prize in a poetry contest.

So one learns that in creative endeavors there is no cut and dried formula for making one's mark. Some writers find a niche early on, others take more time.

Four other former students of mine, who were enrolled in fiction courses and wrote interesting short stories and chapters of novels as class assignments, many years later published successful novels. One of them has won an international award for fiction.

In courses in which I used few or no literary models, generally the first writing assignment I gave was to write an autobiographical piece. This assignment was based on the premise that, if you can write about anything, you should be able to write competently about yourself since you are the authority on that subject! This assignment was also meant to make the point that it is of first importance to tackle a subject you are well-versed in.

The most sophisticated and successful book I know of which resulted from one of my creative writing courses without literary models (though in fact the student was extremely well read with a degree in literature) was a moving family story with autobiographical overtones - a memoir, closely related to a novel. The first draft of this book was written in two graduate creative writing courses during one spring and summer - and refined several times over the years before being published.

Yet despite successes that I know of - and likely others I have not heard of - many of the people who take courses in hopes of producing a successful story, poem, play or piece of creative non-fiction seem unable to do so. Some of these people, who are literate, experienced and seem on first encounter highly qualified to write creatively, cannot in fact do so.

For instance, an astute and well-read medical doctor who took a number of my literature extension courses, producing excellent factual papers, found he could not come up with the fictional pieces he was so keen to write. He told me after class the first evening I assigned topics that he couldn't wait to get started on either a short story or a chapter of a novel.

Because, when speaking or writing down facts, he did so with much charm, lucidity and apparent ease, my expectations of the exceptional fictional piece I was convinced he would produce were high. With the added bonus of his wide medical experience I felt he would have no shortage of insightful subjects to explore.

Not so, as it turned out.

After class the week following the assigning of topics, he told me that he had been trying all week to write a story, and that he just couldn't do it. Pulling a story out of thin air was, he reiterated, an impossibility for him. Hugely disappointed - and surprised - he opted for a conventional essay and as usual produced a first-rate piece of work.

With would-be creative writers like this doctor I have always worried that somehow the in-class atmosphere wasn't right for them, that there was something else I should or could have done to inspire them. Conversely, I find that taking credit for the successful writers who have come out of my courses is not really possible. It seems to me that they would probably have made a success of writing on their own. Since creative writing courses are a fairly modern phenomenon, one has to consider how all the hundreds of wonderful writers in the past who seemingly made it on their own did so - as well as the legions of successful contemporary writers who never enrolled in writing courses.

Seminars can be useful, but the need is great. That's why we are writing this book, to reach a larger audience. Unhappily, though, I think there will always be a sizeable number who won't believe us. They work and work, thinking that they are free of rules and elements of style, but all they accomplish is bigger and deeper pitfalls for themselves. You have to know the rules before you can break them with impunity.

Does anyone remember Anna Russell? She used to sing. She wasn't a bad singer, but when her voice coach told her she didn't have a first-rate voice, she made up her mind to be first-rate bad. She could be very, very bad. Some of the sounds that she could make... But the point is that she had to be good before she could be that bad. She had to know what the rules were before she could break them and turn those broken rules into a very successful career as an entertainer.

Clinton came with a MS that indicated to me that he had a lot to learn. When I had spent an hour teaching him, explaining his mistakes to him, trying to make a writer of him, he said, "Well, I suppose this is just your opinion. I mean, other editors wouldn't necessarily find these things wrong with my MS."

"No, no," I said firmly, without (I hope) letting exasperation appear in my tone, "No, no. These things I've been telling you are the basics. These are the things that every editor looks for."

Here let's stop and explain a little more about editors:

If you look at the titles of editors listed in the reference books, you'll find

Editor-in-Chief

Assistant Editor-in-Chief

Acquisitions Editor

Assistant to the Acquisitions Editor

Senior Editor

Associate Editor

Children's Editor

Non-fiction Editor

Special Projects Editor

and so on...

In this book, of course, we are talking about *book* editors - as distinct from newspaper and magazine editors, etc.

I am a book editor. We are a small firm: I am Editor-in-Chief and Acquisitions Editor. The title I like to use is Acquisitions Editor, which means that I acquire book MSS for my publisher. I decide on my own, or in conference with the publisher and partners,

- whether we want to read your MS
- having read it, whether we want to make you an offer
- when your MS will probably be ready to print
- And, since I also edit adult fiction to printer readiness, I decide whether or not I think we could work harmoniously together.

Remember I told you once before, never show your editor "attitude?" No editor wants to work with a prima donna. I've met a few, not many. But you can be sure I won't choose to work with anyone who seems to be unstable, opinionated to extreme levels, condescending, or unlikely to meet deadlines.

Nancy told me that in all her life she had never heard such nonsense as I was telling her. My reply was, "Not every editor can work with every writer." Nancy had already written several novels, none published. As far as I know, none has been published yet.

Michael looked down his nose at me. Guess what!?

And Florenze didn't send me the MS I said I would read till several months had gone by. Then he told me he didn't... Well, he wasn't going to cooperate with me. He was playing power games, establishing who would be the boss. Guess what!

THERE IS NO SHORTAGE OF ASPIRING WRITERS, BUT PUBLISHERS ARE SCARCE AS HENS' TEETH.

Copy Editors:

You will find many people who work alone and advertise themselves as editors. These people are not book editors. Most of them are copy editors. Some are not much more than first readers.

I am always sorry to hear somebody say, "My MS has been edited." What can I reply? "Oh, yes?"

Usually I ask, "What, exactly, did this editor do for you?"

And usually I hear, "Oh, she corrected all the punctuation and spelling. You'll find it's all correct."

Perhaps I will. But what you had was copy editing, and that was only the last step of what you needed. What are you going to say when I come back in 6 to 8 weeks and say, "You have a good idea here, but it needs a lot of work."

That's when the howls start. "But I paid So-and-so big bucks to edit that... Do you mean..?"

No, what I mean is that you paid a copy editor to clean up your punctuation and spelling before your MS was ready for that stage.

I never ask how much the poor writer paid the editor, but I guess a dollar a page would be bargain basement. And you know now how much you are likely to make on this job, if and when.

MEANWHILE, BACK AT THE OFFICE:

While you wait... While you take long walks and try not to hyperventilate, your editor is juggling 2 ripe tomatoes, 6 sardines (living) a bag of assorted shrapnel, 2 bears, and a hyena. She's getting around to you, reading your offering (and judging it) reporting her findings to her publisher, and writing her letter to you.

She begins her work objectively.

She reads for:

Suitability:

Is the finished book likely to enhance the reputation of the firm?

Leaving aside its theme, has your story flair, style, originality..? Or does it plod along, fairly correct but a little "ho-hum?"

You can't know. You believe you have created the sequel to *Gone with the Wind*; move over Margaret Mitchell. But your editor may be making up her mind to be disappointed; she isn't going to think so.

Are *you* likely to become a star in the firm's crown?

Have *you* originality and style - and a host of other virtues, like health, stability, enthusiasm, energy..?

Margot knows everybody, and the other day, over a cup of coffee at Tim's, she introduced Elizabeth to the very person she needed to meet at that moment.

Perry writes like an angel, but he is so shy he hardly ever opens his mouth; whereas Phyllis glows in the fog.

Yes, we shop around; we have to.

How much work is still needed on your MS
And who will have to do it?

Occasionally a good query letter, an enquiry from a local notable, a referral by one of our writers brings in a MS that should never have come to us, and I feel as I used to feel in my school-teaching days as I tried to think up another inoffensive way of saying to a doting mother: Johnny is a miserable little pest who hasn't learned a thing!

Sometimes a story I thought might be good for us turns out to need so much work I haven't time to take the author on.

Ted did two complete rewrites of his novel, trying to work out the best point of view for the narrator. He worked very hard but did not require much from me. Howard, however, as far as I could see, was going to want me to hold his hand; I couldn't take that assignment. Colin wrote a novel without knowing how to do it; he didn't even thank me for my long letter of advice and encouragement.

BITTER PILL:

Very few editors have time for more than:
We're sorry. Your work is not suitable for
us at this time.
Unsigned
Pre-printed.

Be courteous to the ones who do better than that.
One of my writers needed a jolt of tough love from me. He got it.
His reply began: Everyone tells me I should calm down before I write to
you... Everyone was right. He should have.

Content:

Breathe. You have not heard from the publisher; therefore - probably
- you have passed the suitability test, and the editor has moved on to content. Now she wants to know:

Theme:

Is your theme (really and after all) one that the firm can add to an
existing list of publications on the same or similar themes? Or is it away out in
left field?

Take, for example, *Rising Water*:

Maybe Omni Quinibus *thought* he was writing about a young man who has to come to grips with the inevitability of rising water in the southern Gulf of St. Lawrence - that's what he told me - but I find that he has really written about his relationship with his mother. I am disappointed; we are not interested in mother/son antagonisms; we want rising water.

Plot:

Some authorities say that there is a very small pool (34, or 36, or something like that) of possible plots to choose from. You therefore have to be fresh and original. Are you?

If Omni has written one of these possible plots against the theme of rising water, we *may* be in business.

The rebellion of the younger generation is one possibility. Omni's protagonist will come up against what he sees as the blindness of his parents to on-coming ecological disaster. In the end (according to Omni's query letter) his character will convince his parents, if not to change their ways, at least to allow him to live his life as he feels necessary, without animosity or disappointment on their part.

Or we could have a love triangle. Omni's two girlfriends could fight out the theme as each tries to convince him that her way is best for him and for the southern Gulf.

This is how plot works with theme.

Setting:

Especially if you have chosen to write about the past or the future, the editor will be looking for anomalies: words and expressions that would not have been used by your characters; attitudes that would never have occurred to them; or words and attitudes dragged into the future that don't ring true.

One of the beauties of Lafe Locke's novel for kids, *The Boy Who Wasn't Himself*, is the way he uses speech. Frankie is a Canadian 12-year-old; he talks like one. His double, François, is a French cabin boy, 12 in 1604. François speaks English by literal translation; we never notice that Frankie must be translating his "modern" speech into French.

The Boy Who Wasn't Himself is planned for the 400th. anniversary of the first, ill-fated, French settlement in the New World, which, as everyone knows, occurred in 1604 on a small island in the St. Croix River.

Note: Quite aside from being good, *The Boy Who Wasn't Himself* is topical, always a consideration.

Characters:

Omni is a young man and a young writer. He will probably be able to create a convincing protagonist, whom he describes as like himself; but will he be able to create convincing girlfriends for "himself?"

Believe it or not, I still find girls (in stories) who have the chocolate-box sweetness of the Gibson Girl. I find women like Harriet (Ozzie and Harriet) or like Martha Stewart, who, we have to remember, off-screen has an army of assistants to look after her chickens, frost her cupcakes, and fold her fitted sheets. These female characters are often (not always, but often) the creations of male writers. Maybe they are wishful thinking; they're not "real."

Characterization is specific, of course. You could perhaps have the time of your life making up the story of a 19th c. English school mistress arrived by time warp on Deep Space Nine.

Style:

So if theme, plot, setting, and characters pass muster, the editor enters the subjective realm of *style*, which can be summed up:

Does the way you have told your story serve to bring out the highest potential of your intention? Have you created a work of art? Or not?

The editor's judgment on style can be measured by how many times she calls out to people in the office, "Hey! Listen to this!"

Style has as many points as a porcupine and is about as easy to catch and pin down.

There are the mechanics of style:

spelling

punctuation

grammar

construction

These all count.

There are the harmonies of style:

If Omni's hero is diving in the Bay and is caught in a rip, and Omni writes:

As I fought desperately to rise through a very large wave that all but overwhelmed me, I remembered a day when I was ten - or perhaps twelve years old - when my feet were caught in a bog and I was unable to escape and my mother gave me her hand to pull me out. But my mother would not be able to help me now. I would have to..."

"Oh, Omni!" I would be wailing at this point. "Get on with it, man!

You're in danger of drowning! How do you *feel* about that? How do you *react*? What are you going *to do about it*?"

No, no, Omni. Let's have something like this:

The rip was strong. I fought to keep my head above water. When I could, I gulped air. When I could not, I tried to control my panic, but my lungs were bursting. I knew there was a chance...

Do you feel the difference here? It's what you must strive for. Your reader wants to experience the rip with Omni. *Let him (or her) do that!*

If Omni's two girlfriends come face to face over him... Oh, the possibilities!! They will act according to their own personalities, but the clash will be brief, hands on, and immediate.

We don't want to hear:

Marianne had always been a good girl. Her mother had brought her up to be courteous, considerate of other people's feelings and careful of what she said. It had been a maxim in her family that... because... and so...

Many genre romances are written like that. Boring! Boring! Boring!!

No, this is no time for background - which, I hope, you wouldn't supply by the "had" route anyway. This is a time for Marianne to say, "Greta, you're a nice girl, but you're dead wrong about Omni." Or, "Listen, Greta, I've heard about all I'm going to listen to from you." Or, "Shut up, Greta! For God's sake, SHUT UP NOW!"

Stay in the story and get on with it.

Allison and I could write a whole series of books on style. And we'll have more to say about style.

Enough to say now,

FOR EXAMPLE,

that

- if you are writing in a romantic style, you will use long, soft sounds, words, sentences...
- if you are writing genre romance, you will follow the publishers' rules
- BUT
- that you will impress your own stamp (style) upon it.

And so on for whatever your theme and mood demand. More later.

Very Important Note:

There is sometimes confusion because the word "style" can mean (1) method or (2) the nebulous thing that is your own, personal, individual "take" on all things.

Artistic Appeal:

If your editor reaches this stage and finds that your style, your "presence" is, like the individual pattern of your genes, everywhere but never obtrusive; that it is inducing harmony in every aspect of your writing and in every transition within your MS; that it is... Well, you're probably a reincarnation of James Joyce and your editor will fall on her knees and beg you to let her publish every word you write.

Strive for it. Once in awhile somebody rises to heights like that. Only once in a long while, but we all have to try.

Now, are you feeling a little sick in your stomach because you suspect that, *if you had only known*, you would not have made some of your more egregious errors? Never mind; the editor's assessment is not a life sentence. You can always try again. We will show you more specifics in the very next chapter.

CHAPTER FOUR:

Clarity   Unity   Euphony

Clarity, Unity, and Euphony are the three cardinal virtues of any great work of art. They don't hurt lesser works either.

Clarity:

>Is theme / purpose / *raison d'être* plain to see?
>Is every sentence and paragraph you write unambiguous?
>Does every word you use contribute to the precision of
>the meaning you want to convey?

When I was instructing in the Writing Lab at UNBSJ, students used to come to me with papers marked F, D-, D, and say *I got this bad grade on my essay.* Or *I failed my report. AND I DON'T KNOW WHY* !!!

I would then read the essay, report, whatever it was, with the student, and the conversation often went like this:

"Here's something that may have contributed to your low mark. Look at what you say here."

The student would then read the passage, look up, and stare at me with a perplexed expression.

Perhaps the passage read: *Earth is made of silica.*

I would read the sentence aloud, look up in my turn, and the student's response would be "Yes?" accompanied by the same perplexed expression.

"Is that right?" I would ask.

Back would come the answer, "Yes," but with less conviction.

"Then what do you mean by 'earth?" I would probe.

"Ground."

"And 'made of?"

"Well, it's *in* the ground."

"Silica is."

"Yes."

"But can you say that the ground - all of it (that's what you say here) - is..."

At this point the student would break in with, "Oh, yes, but you know what I mean."

"But that's not what you say."

SAY WHAT YOU MEAN.
SAY WHAT *YOU* MEAN OR *YOU* FAIL.
That might have been my mantra at the Writing Lab.

How this point works:

A new MS arrived today. I had been looking forward to reading it, but my first peek was not encouraging. I read the first 20 pages, and I am still not sure

- who the main character is
- what his problem is
- what the theme or point of the story is
- what mood or tone the writer wants to create.

The only essential ingredient I am sure of is the setting.

But **all these things should have been clear from the very beginning.** (There's a section on beginnings later.)

Here's another example:

Just now I heard a TV news person describe Hans Blix as a "former Swedish diplomat."

I know what the news person meant, because I know who Hans Blix is. But what that news person said is not clear. Questions arise:

Is Hans Blix still Swedish? Can a Swede ever become non-Swedish? Has Hans Blix become a citizen of some other country? If so, can he retain his birth citizenship and be both? Or, does the *former* idea apply to *diplomat* and not to Dr. Blix's citizenship? And what does this speaker mean by *diplomat* anyway? If Hans Blix is not still a diplomat, are we not narrowing the meaning of the word to only *One who is employed by some government for diplomatic purposes?* According to the dictionary, a *diplomat* can be anyone who is tactful and diplomatic, whether employed for that purpose or not.

You see? Vague. Therefore valueless.

Clarity

Clarity

Clarity!

Dear TV Commentator,

If you should ever have occasion to read this book, take heart. I do not mean to set you apart from everyone else and label you the worst, or the only, butcher of the English language. If you seem to come under my fire more often than others, that is only because you are ubiquitous; others have more cover.

While we are at it, however, I have often told students that any night, watching the six o'clock news, I could find at least three examples of what Professor Higgins (*My Fair Lady*) called "the cold-blooded murder of the English tongue," and I have proved that assertion over and over again.

Be clear.

But don't waffle.

Use enough words to make your meaning clear, but not more words than you need. And be sure you know *precisely* what those words mean.

Do NOT write stuff like this:

The bomb dropped on my desk. The day was the day I had been looking forward to. When I wake up most mornings I feel auspicious to see the day. The day the bomb dropped I felt auspicious...

This is not clear. (It is also not a very good example. *You* try being deliberately unclear; it's hard. Which is one reason why we all need editors. We can't do it consciously, but unconsciously we are all capable of saying things that don't make any sense at all, and worse, of reading them over and over again without seeing what is really on the page. Every one of us could type "Hans Blix is a Swedish former" and never notice.)

Note: I know many of you are not used to reading over what you have written. You must learn to do that. You must learn to expect it of yourself. You must persevere until *not* reading what you have written feels as wrong as eating soup with your   fingers. . .

And keep your eyes open for spelling errors, punctuation errors, and typos, as well as for statements that don't say what you mean.

Now. What are the problems in my bomb example? What contributes to its lack of clarity?

- bombs don't drop on desks - not directly, on purpose. So what kind of bomb is this?
- the second sentence is vague and probably unnecessary.
- the third sentence, clear enough in itself, does not clearly connect to the others.
- the fourth sentence rambles and seems to lead to more rambling. I feel a right to expect the last word to be "sad" - anything but "auspicious," which is meant to convey happiness but isn't used correctly; it may mean happy, but not here.

BITTER PILL:

You must not hide important information from your readers. If your narrator or main character knows, the reader should know too.

It is not cute to say on your last page: "Minerva had always known that Rod was unfaithful" when, all along, the reader has thought that Minerva was ignorant of Rod's infidelity.

Or

"Everyone in the village already knew that all the Evanses had a third eye under their hair." Not if the reader has been led to believe that everyone *didn't* know.

Keeping back important facts makes readers mad. They don't laugh, they growl. And since editors are readers... Be clear, open, up-front, and honest.

Clear

Open

Up-front

Honest

"When you have said something, make sure you have said it. The chances of your having said it are only fair."

E.B. White

Unity:

Unity demands that no extraneous matter be allowed in.

BITTER PILL:

Editors can smell padding in a fish-and-chips shop!

Don't pad. (To pad is to add unnecessary details that do nothing but add to the word count.)

Since writers often work to specified lengths - a 2000 word article, a 60,000 word novel - they are sometimes tempted to pad. Don't.

My advice:

If you're writing fiction, add new (relevant) scenes. You can do that. Every storyteller knows far more about his characters than he ever writes down. Add new scenes; don't try to stretch the ones you have.

If you're writing non-fiction, add examples, new points of view, more facts. Never resort to a whole bunch of modifiers - especially adverbs.

***Please* Note:**

> Adverbs should be used sparingly; they'll weaken your work. Stay alert, especially for the ones that end in *ly*. The last thing I do before I decide a piece of work is finished is go through it carefully and remove every adverb that can be cut without spoiling clarity, unity, or euphony. I don't like adverbs;

don't trust them.

To finish what we were saying about unity,

I once attended a day of enrichment for high school English teachers at the University of British Columbia. I remember, now, only that I enjoyed the day but that something was wrong with my car and I couldn't clear the windshield.

That's plain enough. You agree? But what have those facts to do with each other? Nothing much. No unity.

The human mind is not big on unity - at least, mine isn't. I am mentally "busy;" a writer; creative; a teacher used to thinking on her feet and pulling examples out of thin air instantly, on demand; I'm - in a word, to quote my daughters - weird.

If I were to write about that day at UBC clearly in a unified fashion, I would say:

I once attended a day of enrichment for teachers of high school English at the University of British Columbia in Vancouver. I remember, now, only that I heard five or six "talks" but that one stood out from the rest because the speaker, having been allotted one hour, finished in twenty minutes with the words, "Thank you. That's all I have to say." He was clear. His "talk" included no verbiage, no waffling, no "ums" and "ahs;" only enough facts to make his point. Perfect clarity. Perfect unity. *And his words stuck with me.*

CLARITY AND UNITY ARE MADE MANIFEST IN
BREVITY AND SIMPLICITY.
STRIVE FOR THEM.

Euphony:

Euphony is flow, sound, appropriateness of language and construction, harmony in the writing - in a word, music.

Many writers - even experienced ones - fall down on this point.

There is a saying - maybe it is a law - that form and function are two sides of a coin.

Have you ever tried to write an essay that wouldn't come together till you realized it wanted to be a poem? That's this law of form and function at work.

How about a short story that kept on and on till you realized you were writing a novel?

Euphony also appears in your choice of words.

If you say,

On a spring evening in this northern country, tree swallows swoop and soar as they feed on flying insects,

that's euphonious.

Why?

Well, the sentence talks about spring. Spring evenings are long and quiet. In the example, the words used to describe these evenings are long and full of long, quiet sounds.

Look at the vowels:

the e's, for example, in e-e-e-evening and tre-e-e-e and fee-e-e-ed can go on forever, or till the reader runs out of breath.

the o's in aw-aw-aw-on and cah-ah-ah-ahntry...

and the other vowels, all long or long-ish.

The words are long: of 18 words in the sentence, 6 have more than one syllable, as

eve-nings   north-ern
coun-try   swal-lows
fly-ing   in-sects.

And the sentence is slightly alliterative: some of the initial sounds are repeated, as the *s* in swallows swoop and soar, and the *f* in feed on flying insects.

Note: Don't overwork alliteration. It's like cayenne pep-
               per - a little goes a long way.

If we were to describe spring evenings like this (below) the descrip-tion would not be euphonious because the words and sounds would not be appropriate to the job:

After supper, in May, up here in Canada, we can look out the window and see tree swallows flitting and flapping in the air as they eat bugs.

Clear, unified, accurate, but...

Note: If you find you have to use a lot of commas, try
               again.

BITTER PILL:

Euphony is the difference between rolling waves and a short, choppy sea. If you can't feel that difference, I'm afraid you'll never make a writer.

The servants of Clarity, Unity and Euphony:

AS ALLISON SAYS:

TOOLS OF THE TRADE

Before one starts writing, one needs to be in possession of the tools of the trade. The would-be writer has to be literate and grammatical. And although all high school graduates should have mastered these elementary skills, unfortunately this is frequently not the case.

If you send off a sloppy or ungrammatical manuscript to a magazine or book publisher, in all probability the editor who looks at your work won't get beyond the first sentence or two. However good your concepts, chances are that your reader will not keep reading because careless errors are an insuperable barrier for the reader.

To approach writing with the blasé attitude that because you speak a language fluently you can effectively put your thoughts down is unfortunately not true for many people. Close attention to details such as spelling, punctuation, verb and subject agreement, logical unfolding of ideas - usually backed up by lots and lots of practice - is necessary before one can communicate satisfactorily, not to mention brilliantly, using apt and colorful analogies. So, mastering the basics and setting out your piece neatly are essential before sending out a manuscript.

Spelling:

I wish our teaching of the English language had not stopped instructing children that words are made of syllables. The language wouldn't be in such dire straits if more people under the age of 50 had an inkling - even a little one - of how words are put together.

I weep for children who are expected to learn to spell, one letter at a time.
Spell "flabbergasted."
It's not hard, not till you try to do it all of a piece.

In the days before every office had a computer, I once had to type a literature survey: a list of references on a particular subject. They're used constantly when research projects are being designed; that is, if 12 workers have already written papers on the molecular structure of grasshopper spit, the next wants to know what the 12 others had to say before he/she begins to study the spit of grasshoppers that live on the Mistake intervale.

Anyway, when we did my literature survey, we discovered that most writers who came before us were Polish or Hungarian. I shed tears over that job, one letter at a time, one Kleenex tissue per name. Hjkbmztpf at the U. of Nztpznb - you get the picture.

Unfortunately, most - I'm really afraid that most kids nowadays - most kids learn to spell English words like that:
Spell "flabbergasted."
Uh... f-l—a-b(?)... flabe..r... flab
With syllables it's easy: flab - ber - gas - ted. Four of them. All easy to see and - above all - to hear. All you have to remember, really, is that there are two b's in the middle.

And being able to recognize syllables tells you how to pronounce words; they're all in the dictionary.

The word durable, for instance: du-ra-ble. One r means that the u is pronounced long, as in wolf or look; not, as I hear all over the place lately, short: derrable. If it were DERRable, there would be two r's.

But if I ask too much, look at it this way: durable things endure. Right?

Question: Would you say derrable things enderr?

No?

Then why would you say "derrable?"

Answer: I heard it on TV?

Spelling by separate letters leads to mispronouncing all kinds of words: Just last night I heard somebody say,

"The rem-n-ants of" something or other.

The word is – always has been – *rem-nants*.

The rule is – Every syllable has to contain a vowel.

What does it matter? you ask. After all, the language is constantly changing…

So it is, always changing.

If we were to return at the beginning of the 31st. century, we would probably be hard put to understand a word anybody said. But does that mean we should take a chainsaw to the language we have? I don't think so.

I **say preserve the language. Let it evolve; don't hunt it down and slaughter it for pet food.**

Take the word "quickly." Those who know nothing of syllables, who spell letter by letter, are beginning to say *quick-l-y*. Have you heard that? And so what?

Some of you write poetry; you'll understand.

> Quickly, quickly the rain
> Washes the air to a brilliant blue…

How about:

> Quick-l-y, quick-l-y, the rain
> Washes the air…

To my ear, that doesn't work; quick-l-y goes with prick-l-y.

Poets who write humorous verses could play with this strange pronunciation:

> Quick-l-y, quick-l-y
> The prick-l-y pear
> Caught Amanda
> By the hair

> **Poets of the world arise!**
> **Euphony forever!**

You know what Judge Judy says:

> Beauty fades. Dumb is forever.

> But the beauty of the language won't fade as fast if we can avoid words like quick-l-y.

Hyphens:

ANOTHER BITTER PILL:

You will hear that hyphens have gone out of style. *Don't you be-lieve it!*

Hyphens are used to make one word of two – or more. They are guides for the Reader. *Never forget your reader.* It is much easier to read *She wore a pinkish-golden dress* than it is to read *She wore a pinkish golden dress*.

The first one tells you that the writer is attempting to describe a colour that is sort of pink but has gold overtones or undertones or something.

The other one leaves the reader hanging. "She wore a pinkish" – yes, I understand "pinkish" – as much as anybody can. But here's another word: golden. Where does that belong? Does this writer mean it's a dress both pink and golden? Does the writer mean it's a gold-coloured dress but some-times, somehow, appears pink, or vice versa? Or should "golden" be capi-talized because the writer really means to convey that this is a dress designed or made by a person named Golden?

Apostrophes:

Many of you do not know what apostrophes are, what they are for, or how to use them.

If you are one of the many, you know that you are. If you are not, believe me, the many are out there.

Many of the many realize their lack and will admit the problem. The rest believe:

- that apostrophes serve no useful purpose – we don't need them.
- that apostrophes are out of style; therefore it is not necessary to use them.

As I said when we were talking about hyphens: **Don't you believe it!**

Apostrophes are used to show possession: Mary's shoes; Mark's mittens.

"Oh," the many say, "everybody knows…"

But *does* everybody know?

There is a TV commercial these days that shows a sign over a restaurant: Mikes. No apostrophe. What does that sign mean? Meaning is not clear except from the context; we discover, if we bother to watch, that this ad is for a restaurant belonging to somebody called Mike. But I didn't know at first – and I had a perfect right to know – that this was Mike's place, not a restaurant belonging to people called Mikes (pronounced Mee-cash.) You see? Dropping apostrophes leads to confusion, and we already have enough of that!

Apostrophes are also used when writing letters and numbers, as: two 2's are four. The apostrophe is often dropped now, but the dropping whittles away at clarity. If you say: I have an aversion to zs, you will (perhaps) be understood. Qs, not a problem. But as? Watch it! Dropping old rules without thinking about what you are doing is not a good idea.

That is why I have chosen to use the apostrophe in this book. Not because I am old and old-fashioned, but because I am careful to be clear.

P.S. from Allison:

What about apostrophes to indicate missing letters - as in it's = it is? (That's always a hard one, I've found.) So many people seem to think it's is the possessive, confusing the abbreviation with the possessive its.

It's a nice day.
The dog wears its collar.
That looks backwards, but it isn't.

Choosing the Right Word:

Petunia's story was so badly overwritten I laughed out loud. I even read some of her fancier flights to whoever was in the office at the time. Their remarks ranged from, "What?!" to "Is there meaning buried in that somewhere?"

Petunia said things like:

My intrepid forefather in spiritual integrity parted his legs from one another on the littoral torn by tempests of ancient times and bespoke himself into the vomiting air mass rearing white horses on the strand. "Begone," he declaimed. "I will not succumb to your ministrations."

(I made that up but it's not an exaggeration.)

When I told Petunia to write what she meant in plain English, preferably in old words from Anglo Saxon roots rather than in latinate words that entered our language from Norman French... When I said that, she sighed with relief and wrote:

My grandfather, who was very brave, stood on the shore and shouted into the hurricane, "Do your damnedest! My house will stand!"

A lot better, isn't it. At the very least it now means something to a long-suffering reader.

I have high hopes for Petunia.

Note: As a rule, but not always, words from Anglo-Saxon sources are tough and short - the Angles and Saxons were simpler people than the Romans. So, without going into a long dissertation on the history of the English language, if you want simple, strong writing, choose your words from Old English roots. Any good dictionary will tell you.

If you don't understand the *Note:* above, listen to a non-English-speaking singer try to get his tongue around this line:

"When you walk through the storm hold your head up high..."

Nothing hard about that? Not to you. But somebody whose first language is one of the romance (Romanish) languages..? *w* and *h* together? *l* and *k* together! *t-h* and *r* one after the other, going straight into *oo* followed by *gh*? What kind of language is this!? And *s-t-o-r-m*? Not to mention that bunch of *h*'s, one of them with a *g* in front of it?

To them it's as bad as those Hungarian and Polish names were to me. In fact, as a simple rule of thumb, if you find *gh* and *th*, you're into old words. I'm talking about the difference between *death* and *demise*, *think* and *ruminate*, *laughter* and *amusement*. You have to feel them. But until you can, they're all in the dictionary.

Note: Every writer *needs* at least one comprehensive dictionary.

There you have a couple of latinate words: *comprehensive* - complete, full; and *dictionary* - list of words. You need a complete, up-to-date list of English words. And you need to use it. I suppose I refer to mine every day, often more than once. (Allison will tell you that I still can't spell double-barrelled words. There's an example. Is doublebarrelled one word, two words, or does it need a hyphen?)

In Canada our choice of dictionaries is complicated by the split between American English and British English and the fact that Canadians are caught in the middle and use some of each. In the office we accept *Gage's Canadian* as our final authority.

Construction:

Construction: applies to
        sentences
        paragraphs
        chapters
        whole projects:
            essays
            books of non-fiction
            poems
            novels
            short stories
            even picture books.

Your personal style will dictate the construction you will choose, but you can help consciously.

Be watchful. Don't allow yourself to fall into habits you don't even notice.

I once worked with a journalist who was writing a novel – not an easy transition for a journalist to make. This one habitually began sentences with present participles – the *ing* words:

"Sitting on the veranda on a July morning I watched a robin on the lawn. Cocking his head from time to time, he listened for worms and occasionally heard one. Waiting to watch him pull out an extraordinarily long worm, I wondered about being a robin. Hopping around on a mown lawn on a summer morning might be fun, but living on a diet of worms? Hearing the phone ring in the house, I rose, and the robin flew up into a tree."

The journalist had never noticed how monotonous his favourite sentence structure could be.

(There is more about construction in Chapter 7.)

Grammar:

Don't let me start on grammar. That brings us to *authority*.

By whose authority, for example, has the verb *to lay* taken over the verb *to lie* and restricted it to mean *to tell an untruth*? The best English speakers and writers everywhere still say *I was lying on the couch when Heliotrope came in. I* still say *lying*, never *laying around*, **and you should too**. An error is an error, no matter how often it occurs.

When my novel *Red Dragon Square* came out in the year 2000, a newspaper reviewer who was very good to it made only one criticism: that the author didn't seem to know the difference between *lie* and *lay*. I wrote and thanked him for his review and pointed out that it was not I, the author, who didn't know the difference, but Arnold, the narrator, who sometimes (purposely on my part) was mixed up. (Arnold is a young barge worker of limited education.)

The reviewer and I parted on good terms, but the damage had been done: there is no rebuttal to reviews. If anybody at all remembers that review, he or she probably thinks that I am the writer who doesn't know whether she is lying around or - heaven forbid! – *laying* around. So much for reviews.

I tell you that story so you'll know that, as late as the summer of 2000, good writers, editors, and reviewers were still fighting to preserve the distinctions between those two verbs. Yes, I'm old. Yes, I'm fighting a losing battle. But I'm not wrong yet!

One of the most common (among many) grammatical errors is subject/verb agreement - or disagreement!

For example, heard during the war in Iraq:

The grip Saddam Hussein has had around the throats of the Iraqi people are loosening.

Bare Subject of that sentence: *grip*

Complete Subject: *the grip Saddam Hussein has had around the throats of the Iraqi people*

Verb: *are* loosening.

The grip are.

No. The grip is.

Never forget!!!

BITTER PILL:

Since English has no academy to protect it, you will be drawn into battles over points of grammar and usage. As a writer you *must* know the language. Nobody can choose for you whether you will be on the side of the conservatives, who fight rear-guard actions to save words and constructions, or whether you will just go along with the latest vandalism because it is new and easy, and everybody is doing it. But you will have to choose.

Punctuation:

We can't possibly teach you punctuation in a book of this kind, either. We won't even try. Just do as we do – that's one way!

But if you need help – most writers do,

- Find a good, new writer's guide – there are many available.
- Help the kids with their homework.
- Keep your eyes open for punctuation. How do others do it?
- Forget your prejudices. If you go through life muttering, "That's not the way Miss Watson taught us in Grade 4," you're an old stick in the mud. Times change. New methods of punctuation are not wrong if they work. The new ways are generally simpler and facilitate fast, silent reading. If they make the meaning clear, I say, *go for them.*

Note: My approach to changes in punctuation may surprise you. You're right. I rail against changes in spelling and in the meaning of words. But I like modern punctuation. OK?

To Take to Heart:

If you were to copy a short passage from any *good* newspaper, magazine or book *every day*, you would learn punctuation and grammar in no time.

But you won't do that. Too easy.

CHAPTER FIVE:

My MS has been accepted by a publisher. I have a letter of intent; a contract will follow.

CELEBRATE:

Don't ask what you should do *now*. If you have normal nerves and doubts about yourself, you're bubbling with relief and joy. Go ahead. Rejoice. Wow! You're going to be published!

Well, maybe. Celebrate with your first readers. Call your parents and exult with them. But caution the spouse and kids. Unless you want to be

"...one of the people

Running in the race

Buying up the bargains

In the old market place..."

(Remember that one? Stompin' Tom Connors?

"...Spending money we don't got?!")

It's not over yet.

Even small publishers make up their lists a year or two in advance. As I write, at the end of January, DreamCatcher is preparing this year's catalogue. We know whose MSS will become books, in what order, and (we hope) in which month. You expect your editor's time and attention - and you'll have your share - but you will be coming out *next* year.

I am already choosing the titles I will present at the planning session next January. So while I am steering the books for this year through publishing, I am also working with writers who will come out next year, and reading toward the year after that. (One of these years I must remember to retire.)

But you have been chosen. Good for you. Decide with a cool head, because HERE COMES THE WORK!!

My letter to you saying that DreamCatcher is prepared to take your MS to the next level will state clearly what still needs to be done. Look closely and you will find an *if* clause.

Perhaps your letter says,

On the recommendation of our Acquisitions Editor, and having reviewed your MS, the partners in DreamCatcher are delighted with *The Christmas Cactus - in retrospect* and propose placing it on our list for 20—. A contract is enclosed.

You wish!

For one thing, there will be no contract enclosed. What you have is a Letter of Intent, which means that if all goes well your book will be published in 20—. There will be no firm contract till after the meeting in January of that year, when you have demonstrated your ability and willingness to work with your editor till your MS is as good as the two of you can make it.

In the meantime you are obligated not to offer the MS to any other publisher, and the publisher is obligated to keep you on the tentative list for next year but not to assure you that, beyond a shadow of doubt, your book will appear in that or any other year. Otherwise we would not have the term "bumped" in the language, or the old expression, "There's many a slip twixt the cup and the lip."

More likely to come is a letter like this one:

Dear Gerry,

I enjoyed reading *Christmas Cactus*. You have a good story in the making here. But it needs work.

Since your book could be a valuable addition to our line of "green" stories, I can offer you a tentative place on our list for 20—, if you agree to work with ...., who will be your editor, to bring the existing MS to our standards of excellence.

Sounds pretty cold, doesn't it. It is cold. We are saying to you:

Calm down, Gerry. This is a business deal we are offering you, and you have to be calm when you decide whether or not you want to enter into it. (Most writers are so elated by an offer like this they act like a young bat in a swarm of blackflies.)

Go enjoy the moment, but remember:

- the publisher is only taking an option on your MS.
- publication is going to take time and may not come to pass at all; you still have to meet the publisher's requirements - if you can.
- your place on the list for the future is only tentative, and the year of your publication depends on the publisher's resources:

  whether sales of other books are good and the firm makes a

profit.

whether Canada Council or other grants materialize.

whether the publisher has the other resources necessary - qualified people, personal stamina.

whether conditions in the economy in general and the publishing industry in particular hold favourable.

Even fashion...

DreamCatcher had a book - a very good first novel - based on the history of the west coast of Europe in the Middle Ages. Books on that theme had been selling well for several years. We had high hopes. But the bubble of fashion burst during preparation of the MS.

But let's move ahead.

What really happens at a publishing house when an editor goes to work on a MS?

The Book Editor at Work:

The editor goes through your MS again, and blocks it out.

- Does it need to be rewritten or extensively revised?
- How is it for shape?
- Have you remembered your reader?
- Is the narrative voice consistent, or are you constantly sticking in your personal two cents' worth?
- Do you stick to your theme?
- Does the Point of View slide at all?
- Are your characters true to the nature you want them to convey?
- Do the characters speak naturally?
- Is the writing tight enough?

Rewrites:

Let's move rewrites out of the way first.

If the editor decides to suggest a rewrite, she'll send your MS back at this point with comments on serious problems she has found, and with (or without) a promise to read the rewritten version.

Notice what I am going to say next:

My first comments to authors I choose to work with are often...

(Did you catch the key? *I* choose *you*.

Editors choose writers.)

My first comments are often:

You have a great story going here, but you have a lot to learn about story telling. I advise a complete rewrite.

Or

I don't think your MS is working in its present form. It will have to be rewritten.

These comments usually bring groans of disbelief and bleats of protest. Occasionally they bring bursts of enthusiasm that, sadly, usually burn out before long. Once in awhile they bring declarations of determination - they're the responses I like to hear. And sometimes, attacks upon my intelligence, honesty, knowledge, business acumen, age, and sex.

I have been patronized by men. They approach Elizabeth. "Did you know, Mrs. Margaris," they mutter in her ear, "that *she* (meaning me) turned down the business opportunity of a lifetime?" Or, "Elizabeth... (never Betty, though some try) Elizabeth, I was very disappointed in your editor..."

Note: Before you give in to this temptation, be aware that publishers always stand by their people. Publish-

ers know how hard it is to find good editors who
can take the pressures of the business and keep
smiling. Good editors are also scarce as hens' teeth.

Bang your head against a brick wall if you want to. Bury your face in
your pillow and cry - that won't hurt so much. But calm yourself, wait a few
days, then think through your problem.

Do you like your story enough to spend more time on it? Or have you
another in mind?

Can you bring yourself to consider the editor's suggestions? Or do
you prefer to go into denial? (You can always try to find another publisher
and ask for a second opinion.)

You have reached a critical point in your life and career, the point
where art meets business, and it's like... Well, have you seen our Reversing
Falls? Imagine it; reversing falls! Some people - tourists - go through the
gorge in a jet boat. I shudder. I was brought up on horror stories about that
place.

It's sink or swim now. Learn, and learn fast; or let the current sweep
you away into a whirlpool of defeat and disappointment.

Of course, you could have saved yourself all this trouble by learning
how to write first. Think about it!

Earle sent us a novel that was "all but ready to publish." He said it was another *Anna Karenina*. It would make millions. Russian expatriates all over the world would swarm upon it even before it appeared. Here was the opportunity of a lifetime. We should drop everything and pour all our resources into his project. (He only wanted royalties of 25% and an advance of $30,000.) And he was persistent. Give him that.

I turned him down, of course. I was on firm ground. His novel was badly written *and* he wasn't going to work *with* me on it; I was to be his handmaiden in charge of commas - he didn't want to be bothered about them. Otherwise, all we had to do was print the thing and sit back and watch the money tide roll in. He seemed to think we would need a special crew to run back and forth to the bank.

I replied: Sorry, Earle. No. Your MS needs at least two years' work, and I haven't time to give to it, etc.

What!? The MS was ready to print.

Sorry. No. DreamCatcher would not print it as it was. It was not up to our standards.

It was the greatest thing since the old Russian masters!

No. Sorry. It wasn't.

Never a question, like "What's wrong with it?" Even a sneering question, like "What do *you* THINK is wrong with it? You're obviously wrong but I'll humour you." Nothing like that. Complete denial.

Earle tried the divide and conquer route too.

Writers,

It's great to believe in yourself and your work, but editors have their own agendas. Many, like me, also write. Most have their favourite themes, forms, styles, slots in the market. They won't be swayed. If you find one who believes your millions story and agrees to be your slave, beware. You'll pay for that!

Do rewrite if a publisher's editor says you should. You'll learn a lot. But don't think that this suggestion means that your rewritten MS will be accepted for publication automatically. Do rewrite. *But learn how first.*

Enthusiastic writers who work in a lather of passion for their creations will often go off half cocked. They don't wait for instruction to sink in but instantly fly off at some tangent. They have a good story going, but it needs to be rewritten because... They don't wait to see what comes after "because," and the rewritten MS that comes back to the editor is no better than the first one - different, but not better.

Webster wrote a beautiful mother-daughter story. This was in the period when I thought he might learn how to write. But he was like a hummingbird. He would dart in toward me, but his attention would never hold long enough for him to learn. He hadn't done well in school. Therefore...

I could have written the story for him, but then it would have been my story with his name on it. I am not a ghost writer. And he, carried away by his own exuberance, spoiled his first draft, which was good, by changing some of the best parts and adding to the worst.

Rewriting is like working in a garden. If I hire you to weed the tiger lilies, I don't want to come out an hour or two later and find the peonies dug up and laid out on the ground. Rewrite means that you should *re*-write the same story, not that you should write a new one.

Some writers find it hard to stop tinkering and let a MS go to the printer. Even J.R.R. Tolkien, they say, never wanted to part with his MSS. His publisher had to pry them loose from his grasp. Try to develop a sense of proportion about your work. Let it go at last with good grace. Nothing warns an editor of impending disaster like a writer's reluctance to meet deadlines because he wants to think about some sticky point a month or two longer.

No, no. Arrangements for printing, reviews, launches... are made well in advance, so if a publisher says, "We're going to the printer on the fifteenth," that's final. All of us *must* be ready, including you.

Revision:

If the book editor thinks that rewriting is not necessary but that some pretty extensive revisions need to be made, she'll send your MS back with detailed instructions on how to go about this task.

You will be asked to revise certain points, sections, characters. Revision does not usually involve the whole MS.

Note: Revision looks like a lot of work. Often it is a lot of
                  work. Many writers balk at this stage. They feel
                  discouraged, disenchanted, resentful, insulted.
                  Who, after all, is this opinionated person who stands
                  in judgment over the perfect products of their very
                  souls?

The answer to that question is this:

Writer, the person who stands in judgement may be your best friend -

in deep disguise if you like, but your best friend all the same. So if you want to be published...

You may be asked to revise:

Shape:

By shape we mean

- does the action progress from beginning to end in logical order?
- Is there a climax?

    If so, where does it occur?

    If not, why not?
- How much of the length is given to the beginning and the end?
- Is the middle strong enough to hold the reader's interest?

Writing a book is like training for the Olympics. You don't want to peak too soon. But you are working toward a point where what you have to say comes together: your theme is justified, your action grows like a pot coming to the boil until it erupts into activity, your characters are vindicated - or destroyed, and after that your story is over. There will be a little more, but it will be like the hem on a shirt - necessary but shouldn't draw attention to itself.

Flashbacks and Zigzags:

"Flashback" is a recognized term. Everybody knows what it means. You start a story at a point in time; and having established the parameters, you go back to a previous time and describe events that happened then.

Flashbacks are legitimate and very useful. You have to be careful, though, not to confuse your reader. Make sure to be clear. Usually the careful writer leaves a few blank lines to indicate a change in time, which may be a change back to a previous period, or a return forward.

"Zigzags" are a type of flashback. (The term is possibly mine.) By zigzags I mean parts of a story that appear as flashbacks more than once. Usually they add new detail or are told from a different POV. I used them in *Red Dragon Square*. Penner's Rock, for example, is always seen through Arnold's eyes, but he remembers it differently each time he thinks of it.

Flashbacks are not always easy for the reader to follow; zigzags should be used sparingly; but the point to keep in mind is that ***everything must move the story forward***. Don't be tempted to flash back to a point that is – to you – very interesting or impressive, if it does not build part of the road that leads to the climax.

Leading to the Climax:

- No side issues.
- No anecdotes just too good to leave out.
- No wandering away from the theme.

Have you ever driven along a country road and noticed all kinds of interesting lanes and side roads, and said to yourself, *One of these days I must explore..?* That's it. One of these days. But not now. Today we are driving from Point A to Point B, and that's all.

You may have more than one climax, but if you do, they should occur in ascending order of intensity: that is, save the biggest and best for the last. You don't want to have your reader exclaim half way through the book, "But it's over! What's the rest about? Are there two stories in this book?"

Everything leads the story forward to the main climax.

That is what I meant when I said, "HERE COMES THE WORK."

Writing the first draft, revising it to suit yourself, cleaning it up till it satisfies you - that is the fun part. When you begin to work with a book editor, you have to come down to earth and work by your editor's rules, the first of which is:

NEVER FORGET YOUR READER !!!!!!!!

Remembering Your Reader:

Who is your reader anyway?

Will your reader understand this reference?

that expression?

Will your reader be convinced if you say...

this or

that?

Are you sure?

You know how, years afterward, you remember snippets of books you have read or movies you have seen? I have mentioned a movie in which I saw a Granny Smith apple in an otherwise beige control room. I also remember a snippet from Nicholas Monsarrat's novel *The Cruel Sea*, a World

War Two story about the Battle of the Atlantic. I remember that the American captain in charge of an ill-fated convoy sent a message to an escort ship to "ride herd" on stragglers. Immediately, having sent the message, he wondered if the captain of the receiving ship would understand, and just as quickly thought, *Oh, yes. He will. He's a Canadian.* That's what I mean here. You have to keep thinking of your reader.

Of course just about everybody today understands "ride herd," but other expressions... Well... There will be some...

Will your reader understand if you refer to CFB Gagetown and let it go at that? Gagetown, OK. That must be a place. But what about this CFB?

Some readers will become quite wrathy if you use acronyms or abbreviations without explaining them. We have too many nowadays. Every night on the six o'clock news the "disease du jour" is described as Awful Thing That Can Happen To The Unwary *or* LGW.

When talking to experts in various fields who start using their professional shorthand, interviewers will interrupt:

Admiral: Yes. You're right. At JAG we...

Interviewer (murmuring): Judge Advocate General.

Admiral: Yes, yes. At JAG we...

Don't do that to your reader. It doesn't pay. If he probably wouldn't understand your reference, make that reference clear **WITHOUT USING AN I by N**.

Occasionally an opinionated writer will say to me, "If they don't know by now that CFB stands for Canadian Forces Base, they damn well should, and I'm not about to start..."

Oh, yes, you are, if you want readers. *Do* you want readers?

Why *should* I?

Royalties?

Oh.

Words often take on local meanings. I just used one that is fairly common here but not everywhere in this country: *wrathy*. In fact, my computer signalled to me that it did not recognize that word; was it a typo? No, computer, it's a good word - strong - an old word that comes to us from Old English. But like many plants once common in various parts of the country, it has died out in much of the English-speaking world.

How about the word *ugly*? What does that mean to you? *He was some ugly!* Sure. Bad mood. Here, yes. But to most English speakers *ugly* means only unpleasant to look at or hear.

Will your reader be convinced if you write:

One January evening in New Brunswick I was looking out of my window at the Long Reach on the St. John River, and I distinctly saw a giraffe drinking at the water's edge.

To quote Eliza Doolittle, not bloody likely – never, if your reader is a local person. You're more likely to be greeted by guffaws and somebody wanting to know, *Been into the dandelion wine, had you?*

But what if you say:

By the first of January the river was frozen. I was pretty sure the ice was strong enough to bear the weight of a deer or two, but I held my breath when I saw six of them come down to drink.

Eh?!   What?!   Drink?   I thought you said the river was frozen.

Local people won't turn a hair at your assertion. They know all about the places where melt water gathers in puddles under the mid-day sun; all about the places where fast-running brooks enter the mainstream. But if you are writing for a wider audience, you will have to explain or you won't be credible.

But Never Use an I by N.

You'll always miss something. I know - I have the reviews to prove it. But as far as you can, see what is needed and supply it. *Even if you have to sacrifice favourite passages to do it.*

BITTER PILL:

Your editor is always going to want you to cut something you just love. Probably you had better do it. You're entitled to a reason, but do it.

Think.
Decide who your typical reader is.
Write with him or her in mind.

Narrative Voice:

Pay close attention here. This is what I mean by I by N's: Intrusions by the Narrator.

ALLISON SAYS:

James Joyce once said that the author, like the God of creation, should stand back, "paring his fingernails." Certainly, this startling and memorable image emphasizes Joyce's absolute conviction that the writer must distance himself greatly from his creative efforts. But how much distance should there really be? is the question some of us ask.

Particularly in works of fiction (Joyce's primary focus) it is true that the author needs to avoid self-indulgent digressions - getting carried away by extraneous explanations or descriptions, anything in fact which detracts from the forward motion of his story and the development of his characters. Even when his novel or short story is related from a first person perspective, the author should not intrude himself in a recognizable way. It is important to remember that, although a first person narrator may in some respects resemble the author, he is not the author - a mistake both author and reader can sometimes make.

Since I tend to write my fiction from a first person perspective I have had a number of people say "Oh, I know you're writing about what actually happened to you and how you felt." Not exactly!

The eight year old boy who tells his story in Think Like a Goat? is not me, nor is the twenty-something girl in Strange Lights at Midnight, nor the various narrators in Truth to Tell: Stories from Here and Away. But in all these works I have attempted to put myself in these characters' shoes, much, I suppose, as an imaginative actor does - though the actor, unlike the original story-teller, starts with someone else's script.

Although I feel for my disparate characters, and with them, I try to distance myself sufficiently so that I do not personally intrude. Given my characters' situations, I am concerned with having them react in ways which ring true. However, I should add here, that to create believable human beings, the author needs to have known people who in essence resemble them. So I come back to my premise that you can't write about situations or people without knowing where they are coming from - unless, of course, you are writing pure fantasy. But even pure fantasy - such as C.S. Lewis's Narnia narratives, represented by a magical book such as *The Lion, the Witch and the Wardrobe* - needs to have its own internal logic and adhere to its tenets.

In fiction where the author and narrator are much the same age the tie-in is often close - as in Joyce's *Portrait of the Author as a Young Man*, an autobiographical novel. Consequently, the author in his final writing probably should be particularly aware of needing to stand back, of being objective enough to make sure that the work holds together, that he hasn't intruded extraneous and undigested bits and pieces from his own life which at the time of writing seem dear to him but which do not really meld with the story he has set down and will, consequently, divert the reader from the book's real thrust.

This is one reason why in nearly all one's writing it is important to put the supposedly completed manuscript aside for a while (several weeks at least) so that, one hopes, flaws overlooked earlier are now apparent. As well, at this juncture it sometimes helps to solicit the opinion of a trusted friend - someone with first-rate literary skills and appreciation, who also really understands and generally likes your work.

If your friend's view of your final - or all but final - version is critical in part, such criticism is

often hard to take. An adverse view of your manuscript - even parts of it - can be almost as upsetting
as having someone find fault with your child. You
really don't want to hear anything negative, even
if it is the truth! So, it sometimes takes a while to
digest criticism, to evaluate it honestly, and then
decide whether you find it to be valid and consequently worth acting on.

However, when the author is describing something he has done - where his exploits and observations are the essence of the book - the account is
not only going to be related in the first person,
but will probably be "up close and personal." Such
a book is Nova Scotian (Brier Islander) Joshua
Slocum's Sailing Alone Around the World (1900).
Since Slocum was not only a first-rate mariner,
but a witty and to-the-point narrator, his book is
well worth reading.

Slocum, of course, is only one of many successful narrators of first-hand experiences - some book
length (like his) or John McPhee's much lauded
West Coast account of his travels in the North, Coming Into The Country (1977); others, articles such
as many in the National Geographic.

Self-help and how-to books also tend to be related from a first person point of view. This makes
sense, since by and large, the reader isn't going to

consider learning about raising animals or building houses from someone who hasn't had considerable success doing the thing he is discussing.

There are, however, exceptions to this generalization. Medical self-help books are frequently an accumulation of facts which the author has gleaned from various sources, and usually also rely on the writer's own experience. Similarly, books on how to bring up healthy and well-adjusted children and how to achieve successful relationships tend to be gleanings from various sources. Interestingly, authors of these books on relationships, while they may be theoretically knowledgeable about their subject, are frequently not all that successful in their own relationships.

A great many - perhaps most - non-fiction works are not first person accounts, including my own books in this category. Having made use of an accumulation of sources - archival papers, first-hand observations, interviews with appropriate people - the author stands back and writes what he or she hopes is an objective view of the chosen topic. However, as with any other subject the writer touches, he needs to know inside out what he is writing about and care deeply about how he puts together his accumulated knowledge. Such a book needs to be both accurate and readable.

A writer's sources are both exterior and interior. Some writers search the world for suitable landscapes and their inhabitants; others (good poets especially) search their own inner beings. For creative writers of both prose and poetry a combination probably is in order - though I tend to subscribe to Thoreau and Emerson's contention that in questing too far afield one is in danger of depending on travelling as a means of escaping oneself.

To some considerable extent a writer's sources - which he translates into the themes, locations and people which dominate his prose or poetry - reflect his interests and the places he has lived, his powers of observation and the experiences he has had. Frequently, the germ of an idea comes from something or someone the writer has observed with interest - maybe only briefly.

Somerset Maugham has remarked in A Writer's Notebook that in his fiction he has "always needed an incident or a character as a starting point, but," he adds, "I have exercised imagination, invention and a sense of the dramatic to make it something of my own." He goes on to assert, in a colourful analogy, that, although the experience or insight triggering the writer's imaginative response can be slight, it is essential: "There is no need for the writer to eat a whole sheep to be able to tell you what mutton tastes like. It is enough if he eats a cutlet. But he should do that." In other words, the author has to convince the reader that he knows what he is talking about, that even if the work is fiction, it rings true.

For instance, I have for years had a fixation on offshore islands - and of course here in the Maritimes there are scads of islands to consider. Some of my books and stories reflect this fascination. And, as it happens, a good many other people - both Maritimers and visitors - have also been caught up in the subject matter of these books.

Three of my best selling non-fiction books are about islands I have visited off the coasts of New Brunswick and Nova Scotia. These books have been a mixture of fact and folklore, of past and present, of archival material and interviews with island dwellers.

Subsequently, a novel, Strange Lights at Midnight (2003), has an island setting. Although both the island setting and the characters in this book are fictitious, I have had to do with similar people and locations. As well, I had the historical background pretty much at my fingertips, having researched it some years ago for factual books such as Three Remarkable Maritimers (1985) and

Paradise or Purgatory, Island Life in Nova Scotia and New Brunswick (1986).

Two of the stories in *Truth to Tell: Stories from Here and Away* also have island settings, based to some extent on islands I have visited. And although the characters in these stories are fictitious and the islands often a composite, they seem to ring true. A Nova Scotia writer, a friend who read one of these stories, "Never Kid a Kidder", wrote to tell me that he got a charge out of the story and that indeed Archie, the main character, reminded him of a couple of offbeat fellows he'd known over the years.

And then some:

In a minute we are going to edit a little story that will illustrate the remaining elements of storytelling that were listed near the beginning of this chapter (p. 104):

Theme

Sliding Point of View

Presentation of characters

Speech

And in Chapter 7 we'll go after all of them again in a different way – they're that important. But for now...

Copy-editing:

Finally, when all changes have been made, you and your editor must go over the MS once more looking for:

- spelling errors or inconsistencies
- word choices that may not be the best for the specific purpose of a passage, or for the target readership
- punctuation
- name changes.

Believe it or not, the names of your characters will sometimes change in your mind, or you will purposely change them. Take care. You will forget.

I once wrote a novel in which the main female character was called Lindsay. That was fine till a new character turned up, whose name was Alexa. *Alexa* would have done very well, except that other people in the story kept wanting to call her *Lexie*. The names *Lindsay* and *Lexie* were too much alike, so I tried to change *Lexie* to *Allie*. That was very hard, and I wouldn't be surprised to find the odd *Lexie* still in the manuscript. I still think of her as *Lexie*.

Some writers suggest keeping a list of names of characters pinned to the wall where you work. You will forget - if not the name itself, sometimes the spelling.

CELEBRATE AGAIN:

Rejoice. The hard, heart-wrenching work has been finished.
We are going to the printer.

Relax.

Reappraise the situation.

And learn from the little story that follows.

Do not slide lightly over the rest of this chapter. Here you have guidance that reaches down to the bone and sinew of the craft of storytelling. Mark, learn, and inwardly digest.

Note: Never mind the bracketed numbers and letters; they will reveal themselves later.

The Day of the Spruce

During the winter - I believe it was the year 1986 - a tree fell against our garden fence. It was an old spruce. We estimated from its length and its growth rings that it must be over a hundred years old, possibly as much as a hundred and twenty. (1) Spruce trees are listed in the New Brunswick Tree Growers Guide (Government of New Brunswick, Department of Natural Resources, Forestry Division, Pamphlet 128, 1987) as Sprucus New Brunswickus greenus reallybiggus. My wife and I were saddened by the death of the tree.

"I feel the loss of this tree deeply," I said to Veronica as we stood in the window (a) of our newly-decorated living room viewing the wreckage.

"I understand, dear," she replied, and a sense of deep sorrow claimed her heart. "It is not every day that one loses such an old friend," she said. "But, hark! What is this I hear?"

With a hand to my ear I listened. (2) It is a fact well known in medical circles that most people have been slightly deaf since they had measles at the age of ten; hence my hand to my ear. A low moaning was discernible.

"I wonder," Veronica cried, feeling a sudden shudder in her soul. "Could it be..?"

"I do believe..," I replied, (b) remembering the occasion when I was unlucky enough to come upon an accident in the forest.

In a trice we ran out into the snow, expecting to see someone or some animal crushed by the fallen tree.

It was a truck coming down the road past our house that was making the strange sound.

(c) Veronica and I went back to the house and put on a pot of coffee, which we drank with cream and sugar when Pat and Will came in.

"I think we should not drink so much coffee," Veronica snapped. Reaction to these events had taken hold of her stomach.

(3) "Did you know that the average New Brunswicker drinks 125 pounds of coffee beans per year?" Will asked.

(d) I agreed, but I felt I could not do without my brew, and a sense of deep bereavement entered my mind. My coffee too? Was not the tree enough?

That was why, when we stood in the same window five years later, watching a lightning-started fire burn a hundred acres of hardwood across the river - (4) lightning starts 60% of all forest fires around here - that we remembered the winter day the spruce fell, for Spruce was with us. He still limps a little and will never leave Veronica's side during a storm of any kind.

Note: You are free to say that "The Day of the Spruce" is
              the absolute worst short story you have ever read.
              I hope it is. I have laboured long and hard to make
              it as bad as I can.

We will now play "Editors" and go to work on this story.

Shape:
  Beginning - Middle - End

I'd say the beginning of this story ends with "My wife and I were saddened by the death of the tree."

I can see much that is wrong with this beginning, but it is not out-of-proportion long for the rest of the story.

Now let's look at the end.

Oh, oh! What on earth is this about? It doesn't seem to have anything to do with the beginning and does not, apparently, grow out of the body of the piece, which, at this point, is talking about coffee. Ooo! This writer has problems. The end is not, however, out of proportion with overall length.

So now we'll read the whole story looking for the climax and denouement.

We begin. We read on into the action. We rise to the point where "I" and Veronica rush out into the snow. And then we tear out our hair and scream, *What's going on here? WHERE IS THE CLIMAX?*

Note: Lack of climax sometimes means that the writer wants an anti-climax; that is, nothing appropriate happens, or something humourous happens - a silly twist. An anti-climax comes at the very end of a story, most commonly in anecdotes where the teller of the tale wants his audience to laugh. Anti-climaxes also occur - occasionally - in short stories. They even occur, though rarely, in novels (for example, *Fiasco* by Stanislaw Lem.)

But an anti-climax in definitely NOT wanted here.

"The Day of the Spruce" falls like a souffle. Where there should be a nice, round top, it has a deep hole. And you have every right to roar, "What did they find under the damn tree?"

Shape, therefore, like a road, has to do with length (and the natural divisions of finite length) and with the ups and downs of altitude.

Have you ever driven from Saint John to Montreal by the Canadian route? There's the long beginning up the valley of the St. John River, which does, at least, twist and turn a bit and have its ups and downs through the hills; then there's an endless (to me) slog up the St. Lawrence Valley, where the road is flat and pretty straight, and seems to go on forever; and finally the relief and expectancy of the city looming in the distance. Through a tunnel or over a bridge, and you're there!

As a blue print for a short story, that road is only fair. The beginning is too long, the middle too flat, the climax too abrupt, and the denouement short. But I hope you see the plan.

Now let's try to revise "The Day of the Spruce."

We will have to add something after *It was a truck coming down the road past our house that was making the strange sound.* We'll try *But under the tree, caught among the branches, was a half-grown puppy. He was not hurt, but he was shivering and whimpering, and he yelped for joy when he saw us.*

Now the story has a climax.

But... Oh, boy! This story has problems! How to solve them!!!

Theme:

What is this story about? Is there a point to it? Why did the writer think it was worth telling?

What do *you* think the theme is? **Try to figure it out *before* you read what *I* think it is.**

I suspect that the theme of "The Day of the Spruce" has something to do with loss and recompense: when one door closes another opens. The loss of the tree leads to the gain of the puppy.

But theme isn't clear in this story.

So how do we make it clear?

First we delete everything that wanders from the theme. This part is fun (for me) but some students have called me Mrs. Chop Chop. Often there isn't much left when the waffling and extraneous material have gone. Deletions are in italics in Version 2.

The Day of the Spruce, Version 2

During the winter - *I believe it was the year 1986* - a tree fell against our garden fence. It was an old spruce. We estimated from its length and its growth rings that it must be over a hundred years old, possibly as much as a hundred and twenty. *(1) Spruce trees are listed in the New Brunswick Tree Growers Guide (Government of New Brunswick, Department of Natural Resources, Forestry Division, Pamphlet 128, 1987) as Sprucus New Brunswickus greenus reallybiggus.* My wife and I were saddened by the death of the tree.

"I feel the loss of this tree deeply," I said to Veronica as we stood in the window *(a) of our newly-decorated living room* viewing the wreckage.

"I understand, dear," she replied, and a sense of deep sorrow claimed her heart. "It is not every day that one loses such an old friend," she said. "But, hark! What is this I hear?"

With a hand to my ear I listened. *(2) It is a fact well known in medical circles that most people have been slightly deaf since they had measles at the age of ten; hence my hand to my ear.* A low moaning was discernible.

"I wonder," Veronica cried, feeling a sudden shudder in her soul. "Could it be..?"

"I do believe...," I replied, *(b) remembering the occasion when I was unlucky enough to come upon an accident in the forest.*

In a trice we ran out into the snow, expecting to see someone or some animal crushed by the fallen tree.

It was a truck coming down the road past our house that was making the strange sound. But under the tree, caught among the branches, was a half-grown puppy. He was not hurt, but he was shivering and whimpering, and he yelped for joy when he saw us.

(c) Veronica and I went back to the house and put on a pot of coffee, which we drank with cream and sugar when Pat and Will came in.

"I think we should not drink so much coffee," Veronica snapped. Reaction to these events had taken hold of her stomach.

(3) "Did you know that the average New Brunswicker drinks 125 pounds of coffee beans per year?" Will asked.

(d) I agreed, but I felt I could not do without my brew, and a sense of deep bereavement entered my mind. My coffee too? Was not the tree enough?

That was why, when we stood in the same window five years later, watching a lightning-started fire burn a hundred acres of hardwood across the river - *(4) lightning starts 60% of all forest fires around here* - that we remembered the winter day the spruce fell, for Spruce was with us. He still limps a little and will never leave Veronica's side during a storm of any kind.

The Day of the Spruce – Version 2 after cuts

During the winter a tree fell against our garden fence. It was an old spruce. We estimated from its length and its growth rings that it must be over a hundred years old, possibly as much as a hundred and twenty. My wife and I were saddened by the death of the tree.

"I feel the loss of this tree deeply," I said to Veronica as we stood in the window viewing the wreckage.

"I understand, dear," she replied, and a sense of deep sorrow claimed her heart. "It is not every day that one loses such an old friend," she said. "But, hark! What is this I hear?"

With a hand to my ear I listened. A low moaning was discernible.

"I wonder," Veronica cried, feeling a sudden shudder in her soul. "Could it be..?"

"I do believe..," I replied.

In a trice we ran out into the snow, expecting to see someone or some animal crushed by the fallen tree.

It was a truck coming down the road past our house that was making the strange sound. But under the tree, caught among the branches, was a half-grown puppy. He was not hurt, but he was shivering and whimpering, and he yelped for joy when he saw us.

That was why, when we stood in the same window five years later, watching a lightning-started fire burn a hundred acres of hardwood across the river, that we remembered the winter day the spruce fell, for Spruce was with us. He still limps a little and will never leave Veronica's side during a storm of any kind.

Ah! Now the theme is beginning to come clear.

Intrusions by the Narrator (I by N's)

Look back at the first version of our story and you will notice that I cut two types of material. Some cut passages are definitely I by N's and *must* go. You will never convince me that you should keep them. Nobody wants to be lectured to as he reads. You probably know people who do that in conversation. Boring people. They're I by N's in human form. I have numbered those passages 1, 2, 3, and 4. Without them the story flows better. Doesn't it!

The parts marked a, b, c, and d are debatable. If you really want them, you'll have to convince me that you can link them to the theme. But it would be possible to convince me.

Sliding POV:

Yes, the POV slides. If this story went on long enough, readers would begin to think they were watching a tennis match; and some with sensitive constitutions might feel nauseated.

In a short story, there is generally only one POV character. In "The Day of the Spruce," that character has to be the first-person narrator, which means that the author may report only what that character is thinking and feeling, because the author is sitting in his head and watching the action through his eyes.

The author must not report what Veronica is thinking and feeling unless she tells him by what she says or does – language or body language.

The author must not hop from one head to another. Head-hopping constitutes sliding POV. Bad. Very bad.

Note: In long short stories that are told in the third person, the POV sometimes must be shared between two characters - even (rarely) among three or more - BUT only at scene breaks.

The Day of the Spruce, Version 3

Note: Italics in this version show POV corrections. Compare them to the previous two versions.

During the winter a tree fell against our garden fence. It was an old spruce. We estimated from its length and its growth rings that it must be over a hundred years old, possibly as much as a hundred and twenty. My wife and I were saddened by the death of the tree.

"I feel the loss of this tree deeply," I said to Veronica as we stood in the window viewing the wreckage.

"I understand, dear," she replied, and *I could tell by her face that* a sense of deep sorrow claimed her heart.

"It is not every day that one loses such an old friend," she said. "But, hark! What is this I hear?"

With a hand to my ear I listened. A low moaning was discerned.

"I wonder," Veronica cried, *looking as if* a sudden shudder *had seized* her soul. "Could it be..?"

"I do believe..," I replied.

In a trice we ran out into the snow, expecting to see someone or some animal crushed by the fallen tree.

It was a truck coming down the road past our house that was making the strange sound. But under the tree, caught among the branches, was a half-grown puppy. He was not hurt, but he was shivering and whimpering, and he yelped for joy when he saw us.

That was why, when we stood in the same window five years later, watching a lightning-started fire burn a hundred acres of hardwood across the river that we remembered the winter day the spruce fell, for Spruce was with us. He still limps a little and will never leave Veronica's side during a storm of any kind.

Next,

Do the characters act naturally?

The characters are pretty true to their (to me) boring, middle-aged selves. But I would not say that Veronica "snapped." Veronica seems pretty sappy; I don't think she would snap.

Do the characters speak naturally?

Uh-uh! They do not. But, do you know, there are still people - and they aren't all old - who think that this Mary Pickford-type speech of the silent film era is the way to write?

No, no. Please. Nobody says "hark!" anymore. Or "in a trice" or "I do believe."

We will now make the characters speak naturally:

"Aw, this is a shame," I groaned.

"It's like losing an old friend," Veronica said. "But listen. There's something... Can you hear it?"

"You may be right," I cried.

Is the writing tight enough?

Tightness in writing is like tightness in knitting.

Some people are loose knitters. They hold their yarn and needles loosely, which results in fabrics that are soft and drape easily, regardless of the bulk of the yarn or the size of the needles, but that are also full of holes - the wind blows right through them. Others knit so tightly that everything they make is hard, and stiff as a board.

Your writing style will be like that. Try for the happy medium. If you are too loose, your editor will tell you to prune back some of the excess - words, paragraphs, illustrations... If too tight, she will suggest that you loosen up - make some longer sentences, add a simile or two, expand an idea.

PLEASE REMEMBER:

This phase of the editing is where you will learn that I am not trying to impose my style on you but only trying to teach you effective method. This point will come up again.

Now that we have cleaned up the obvious difficulties - the points of theme and presentation that, if not corrected, would detract from the story and spoil the writing - we can consider the rest of the places where cuts or changes might mean improvement.

If this were my story,

1.   I would take out *I believe it was the year 1986.* That would be my choice. My style is spare - cut to the bone. But if your style is chatty, discursive, keep that information if you want it.

2.   I like to cut all unnecessary words, so I'll choose to say *During the winter an old spruce fell against our garden fence,* and save four words.

When you read my final version, you'll see my style being imposed upon the story. But *before you read it, you would profit from writing your own version*, to impose *your* style upon *The Day of the Spruce* before the possibility of influence by mine enters the picture.

3.   The passive voice of verbs is always weaker than the active voice:

> *A low moaning was discerned* is passive.

Find out about Active and Passive. This is not a grammar text so I'm not going to go into that here, but you should know. It's the difference between:

> *I ate an apple.* Active. Strong.
> And *An apple was eaten by me.* Passive. Weak.

Sometimes you can't escape the passive because only the passive form will fit. Some verbs have only passive voice. But as a general rule:

Prefer Active Voice of verbs over Passive.

4.   Too many characters spoil a short story. I'd delete Pat and Will. But the choice is yours.

5.   For the sake of the story, I would begin with the fire and look back to the tree.

6.   I would change the title to better suit the theme.

You'll see all this when you read the final version.

Copy Editing:

Finally we check

Spelling.

You are free to choose British or American spelling. Just be consistent.

Punctuation.

If you are bright-eyed, you have observed that sometimes Allison and I don't seem to follow the same rules of punctuation. Styles differ. None is either right or wrong - except where a certain style is required, as, for example, in papers written for the nursing profession.

Punctuation exists for the guidance of the reader. Therefore be clear and consistent.

Word Choices.

Words have dictionary meanings. Stick to them. Characters in

Wonderland could use words to mean anything they liked, but even Alice had a hard time with that. Your readers will have an even harder time if you use words to mean what you want them to mean - not what everybody else knows they mean.

And please don't fall for the computer-generated, "simplified" language some people are using. Those people think they are up to date, even avant-garde. I hope not. No person, let alone a computer program, can foresee all the effects of changing the meaning of a word. Most of these changes come from ignorance and lead to confusion, to blunting the edge of the beautiful tool that is the English language.

For example, a senior editor of a new dictionary for American high school and university students accepts a change in the meaning of the word *unique* to include *different.* She says that the new dictionary will point out to students that *unique* means, of course, *one of a kind*, but that, since it is now commonly (even if erroneously) used to mean *different*, the dictionary will direct users to choose the *new* meaning in everyday speech and writing, but to remember that they must restrict *unique* to *one of a kind* when writing school papers.

That, to me, looks like confusion – worse, to the loss from the language of a word that means (specifically and only) *one of a kind*. Since I agree with Professor Strunk (Strunk and White, *Elements of Style*), that we should never use several words where one will do, I naturally feel deeply the loss of the word *unique*.

Or, if you want a shorter example, the other night I heard an interviewer ask an expert on world affairs, if the *opticed* (pronounced "op-tick-ed") account of something or other... I cheered when the person interviewed said, "I don't know what you mean by *opticed*." Many people would have confounded confusion by pretending they knew this meaningless word. That's what I mean when I keep yelling **ON WHOSE AUTHORITY?**

Accuracy

Allison and I have been dealing with accuracy all through this book.

Use accurate data,

accurate words,

accurate constructions.

If you need an example of what I mean by accurate construction, consider this:

Being the biggest storm of the year, he put on his warmest coat.

This is an example of that old cry, "Oh, but you know what I mean." Sure I do, but if you make mistakes like that, I'll wonder, **do YOU?**

We have a long list of suspect words and constructions. We've seen a few. But how about:

- frustrated   Did you know that this word does *not* mean angry?

  No more than
- paranoid   means what you probably think it means.

- One thing I like about birds are their feathers. How can anyone reach the plural verb "are" having started from "*one* thing?"
- One of my family's favorites is:

  I have a solid-rock maple dining table.
- Or...   They live in an apartment above a store on the third floor.

HERE IS MY FINAL, EDITED VERSION OF
The Day of the Spruce

New title:

When the Tree Falls

Veronica and I stood in the window and watched a forest fire destroy a hundred acres or so of hardwood forest across the river. Spruce, our half-bred German shepherd/husky, was with us and never left Veronica's side. He never does when there's trouble about.

"Never mind, Spruce," Veronica said, as she laid her hand on his head. "Never mind, boy. It's sad that we have to lose those beautiful trees, but something else will come up. Maybe the people will farm blueberries instead. I guess you can't see colour, but you can take it from me, there is hardly a colour in the world more beautiful than a blueberry field in autumn."

Spruce never took his eyes from Veronica's face. He thumped the floor - just a little - with his tail, but he didn't look away, or look convinced.

My mind went back to the day, six winters before, when an old spruce tree came down across our garden fence and Veronica and I ran to this same window to look out at the wreckage.

"Aw, this is a damn shame!" I groaned. "That was a good old tree."

"It's like losing an old friend," Veronica agreed. "I... But listen! Can you hear something?"

"Yes!" I exclaimed. "I do hear something."

We pulled on our boots and ran out into the snow. A low moaning sound - the sound we had heard through the window - was louder there and obviously only the noise of a truck coming along the road. But there was another sound, a whining, barking, yipping sound that we couldn't have heard from inside the house.

We leapt through drifts of snow toward the fallen tree, and there was a half-grown puppy appealing to us for help. Shock and terror filled his eyes. He tried to wag his tail, but it was caught between bits of broken fence and the fallen trunk of the tree.

Veronica laughed when we had freed him and he began to leap and caper around her.

"Well, here you are," she said, as she scooped him up in her arms. "You're just the puppy I've been needing all winter long. Let's hurry in out of the cold. I'm freezing and you must be too."

While I cleared away the snow and twigs we tracked into the house, Veronica placed a bowl of fresh water on the floor for the pup. She also put on the coffee pot for us. But she never took her eyes off Spruce.

After his drink, Spruce settled down in a warm spot beside the wood stove, and never took his eyes off Veronica.

Spruce has been with us ever since, and we hope he'll be with us for a long time to come, to stand guard over Veronica, and to help us watch the blueberry field across the river when it turns from green to autumn rose - even if he can't see colours.

CHAPTER SIX:

The Reasons Why
   Why we must promote ourselves and our work
   and some ways to do it.

Book buyers will pay top price for the latest self-help books: we are all going to improve our lives, and the sooner the better. If you can write self-help, you may just clear your million.

Book buyers will pay for "must-have" hobby books. Take cook books. If you want to sell copies of your work fast, a good cook book with a hard cover and pages that lie flat, with lots of coloured illustrations and how-to instructions will do it.

You probably know this. You've probably bought cookery books yourself. I used to. Before I decided I was not much of a cook and even less a baker, and gave most of my cookbooks away, I had shelves of them.

And knitting books! Those I bought and used. I made sweaters before I started writing and editing full time and had plenty of finger exercise typing. I would pounce upon a bright new knitting book, never mind the cost - $50, $60, $75... There was no logic to it. I could knit, perhaps, five sweaters a year. Every knitting book I bought held patterns for five years at that rate, not counting the variations that could be rung on a single pattern with changes of colour, bulk and texture. Still I bought and bought, and waited eagerly for each month's knitting magazines to appear.

At the same time, like everybody else, I bought fiction in second-hand stores - and still do. My heart bleeds for my fellow authors, but still... Well, you know, I'd never get them read. With all the MSS I read, my eyes...

But at Christmas I bought *for myself* two special new volumes of non-fiction:

> *Walking in This World* by Julia Cameron (in hard cover!)
> and *Take Time for Your Life* by Cheryl Richardson.

Julia Cameron is one of my favourite writers on writing and the writing life. I recommend that you read her. No, I *strongly recommend.*

Cheryl Richardson really does inspire people (at least, me) to keep New Year's resolutions for a few days.

The truth is… Here we go again:

Buyers of fiction are usually women, usually between 25 and 60, and they shop for fiction as they shop for vegetables - in bulk, so much a pound; occasionally to add a little spice; and only what they need for the next few days. They might as well be buying cabbage, varied once in awhile with Brussels sprouts.

Some people are swamped with reading - at work - at church - at school.

When I complained that the members of my church didn't seem interested in one of my books when I thought they should have been, one of them replied that they all had a basketful of obligatory reading already. And no time for my perspective? Apparently not.

Some people don't like to read. Most would rather find entertainment (which they think fiction always is) on TV, the Internet, Videos, radio... Sure. OK. "Amongst them be it," as my grandmother used to say. Don't let it bother you.

Note: When you have subtracted all the people who can't read, can't read English, never read, don't want to read, and hate sharks, there are still millions left. It's just that you are unknown to them. They are busy. And nobody can feed books to the cat or run the car on them. Those readers will wait till you show up in the second-hand store. But they will read you - eventually. Meanwhile you'll be writing your next book. Because you are a writer.

Publishing is business. I keep hammering this point. And most of the business of publishing is promotion. Not buying and selling. Not even advertising, though that's important. Promotion is the key. Giving the buyer in a saturated market a product (ugly word) that she wants. And keeping your name and face before her all the time.

ALLISON SAYS:

Long ago I used to think that getting a book published was the final hurdle, that if the book was well written and interesting it was bound to receive the favourable attention and devoted readership it deserved - maybe not at first, but sooner or later. With the writing of the book, the author's work, I assumed, had been accomplished.

Not really true. I was naive. The writer still has to participate in publicizing his or her book. The book has to sell.

Indeed, in this age and part of the world, there is a surfeit of all kinds of 'products' - literary ones included - competing with one another, and without the right kind of publicity none of them is going to sell. Although it is mostly up to the publisher to arrange for suitable publicity for the volumes he puts out, the writer has to do his part - particularly if the book is published by a small press, since such presses frequently lack the resources for advertizing.

The publisher usually sees that the book is reviewed and arranges for book launchings, signings and interviews, but the author has to be there, ready to participate. To some extent as well, he or she has to be available to speak to various groups who express interest in the current book and/or its author.

Book signings mostly occur in stores where the writer is slated to appear for that specific purpose. I have always been surprised by how variable and unpredictable such signings are.

Over a usual two hour stint in a particular store, I've had as few as two people, and as many as one hundred and fifty, turn up. While taking into account the place, the time, and of course the book, I have never been able to figure out just why some signings are so successful, others a waste of time.

Even in stores where the book is consistently selling well, people do not necessarily show up at the designated time to buy their copies and have them signed - though that doesn't mean they don't care whether or not the copy is signed: they not infrequently contact the author later to see if she will sign their books. Either they didn't know about the signing (poor publicity - or none), they had other plans at the allocated hours, or they simply didn't feel like an outing at that specific time. Who knows....

Book launchings, in my experience, are variable and depend on a surprising number of factors which are not as closely related to the author and the book being publicized as an inexperienced person might think. Entering significantly into the picture are the prestige of the sponsor, the place, the time of year and time of day, the weather - and although lots of people wouldn't admit to being drawn in by such a consideration - the food and drink being served. Then, it is of prime importance to realize that, no matter how perfect all these arrangements, the launching will probably fail without a lot of the right kind of persistent public relations advertizing - work done well in advance of the event and continuing right up until it is scheduled to begin.

Apart from a book's publisher, others who sometimes launch an author's work are: a university with which the author is intimately connected, a library, a society which is interested in sponsoring either the author or the book (preferably both), or even the person the book is about, if it happens to be a contemporary biography. I have been fortunate in having had some memorable launchings under all these auspices.

During the twenty years I taught at the Université de Moncton, the university gave my literary efforts its full and continuous support - including two very successful launchings in the large and elegant salon bleu. A former student of mine, then working for the university's Public Relations Department, masterminded both these launchings, which were several years apart. On these occasions, friends spoke on my behalf, the media did interviews, people chatted easily while waiters with trays of wine and cheese circulated through the crowd - and my publishers (not the same ones in both instances) sold a lot of books.

For several other books, the Moncton Public Library, with the assistance of the Canada Council, sponsored two successful launchings. The first, arranged by one of the librarians, again one of my former students, coincided with the opening of the new city and regional library in the then-just-built Blue Cross Building. Two writers, one Anglophone, one Francophone were invited to read in different places at different times. As the Anglophone author, I was asked to give a reading not only in Moncton but in several of the predominantly English-speaking communities nearby. The Moncton reading was so well advertized - right up to the last moment - that the room was packed.

The other well-attended launching/reading, with the same sponsors, was to celebrate the publication of Poetic Voices of the Maritimes, a collection of regional poetry which a friend, Dr. Theresia Quigley, and I had put together. Four of the poets included in this book gave readings. This launching, like the others just mentioned, took place in the early evening.

The only really successful afternoon launching of my books was given jointly by the Parrsboro Geological Institute and the Parrsboro Historical Society. They launched my two Gesner books - for very good reasons. Although Nova Scotia born Abraham Gesner was Canada's first geologist, and New Brunswick's first official geologist, having been employed by the New Brunswick Government for four years, he had lived in Parrsboro, practising medicine there, while exploring the Fundy shore's rich geological formations in all the spare time he could manage.

The launching, in the beautiful, and then just newly-built Geological Institute, was crowded with local residents as well as a good many people from 'away'. It was also attended by the media, who subsequently publicized the event. After the launching, I was driven in state, in a restored vintage automobile, to an elegant tea, served in a lovely and historically significant old house by the sea which the Historical Society has been restoring over the years. I was treated like royalty - and lots of books were sold at both locations.

A totally different type of launching from those just cited was given by Maritime music stars Ivan and Vivian Hicks to celebrate the publication of my biography *Ivan Hicks: Fifty Years of Fabulous Fiddle Music.* Ivan and Vivian had hired a professional to organize and publicize the event. She did a terrific job. The large crowd was treated to an evening of great fiddle music, interspersed with a few short speeches by the mayors of Moncton and Riverview, the lieutenant governor, a colleague of mine and myself.

The mood of those in attendance was upbeat and relaxed. Now and then a few people, unrehearsed, got up spontaneously and step danced to the music. Others called out requests for tunes they wanted to hear. During the breaks people chatted with friends, bought books and helped themselves to the splendid feast - a buffet laid out on large tables and replenished frequently.

The most unusual, and one of the most successful bits of publicity I've had to do with was when the publisher of Offshore Islands organized an island tour. (This was a year after the book first appeared, by which time it had had an excellent review by the former publisher of the Chronicle Herald, Harold Shea, and had been on that newspaper's list of regional best sellers for eight months.) The first forty plus people who signed up spent a week travelling to various destinations near islands, staying overnight at the best accommodations the region afforded, and then, when weather and fishermen cooperated, going by boat to a few of the islands I had written about. My husband (who had illustrated the book) and I were invited to travel with the group, and I had agreed to give frequent talks about the various islands.

The trip, which had been well planned and well publicized, was a success. In fact, as my publisher told me, he had received queries about it from so many other people who were eager to be included that a whole convoy of buses and boats could have taken an eager public to these special places. That Offshore Islands went through seven printings was very likely a tribute to the effectiveness of this sort of publicity.

Many authors - perhaps most - cringe at the thought of promoting themselves. They're - most of them - solitary by nature and habit, and already mentally in the world of their next book. They don't *want* to go out and speak in public, sign books, "make nice" with a bunch of strangers. They don't even want to go out with friends just for fun. When *Come to Say Good-bye* was going great at about Chapter Six, one of our writers had an important birthday - one with a zero. I enjoyed the party very much when I was there, but Elizabeth and Rosita, who was with us then, had to drag me out of my apartment. I was howling inside like a kid of four - *No, Mamma. I don't want to. No-o-o-o-o-o!!!*

Don't worry. Self-promotion comes in many easy ways that you can practise daily.

- Be seen in your neighbourhoods - where you live, where you work, where you play, worship, eat... And, *this is important*, always look approachable. As your mother used to say, don't slouch, pick up your feet, and if anybody gives you a chance, smile, nod, say hello. Say it so you can be   heard. Smile so your smile can be seen. It's easy. Just don't be shy - writers often are; I suppose it has something to do with the solitary lifestyle.

A couple of years ago I dropped in for lunch at a restaurant in the neighbourhood where I live. A waiter took my order, but the owner, who knows me, brought my meal. She wanted a chance to whisper to me, "See that man at the table by the cactus? That's ——— ———. I thought you'd be interested."

I was. A writer of his calibre? You bet! But all I ever saw of that man was the back of his head and the slope of his shoulders. He sat with his back to the room (though he was alone) and didn't speak a word, not even to the waiters.

I suppose when you are as well known as he, you don't have to let people see your face. But that's not for you. You can't afford that privacy - yet.

Who knows what might have happened if that well-known face had been turned toward the room. I, for one, would have felt moved to buy the book he was in town to sign. I didn't. Only one sale, you say? Yet a sale is a sale - a couple of dollars just for showing the front of your head? Think what a smile could do.

And, you know, I'm not even sure of his name now. It may have been ——— ——— but maybe not; possibly ——— ———. What if he had looked at me? Or given me a nod, or ten seconds of his time? I would have been dropping his name all over town.

- Talk to people - the milkman, the paper girl, your hair dresser, the guy at Tim's, the lady at the Post Office. It doesn't hurt, and it will pay dividends for your writing as well as for your "profile."

A word of warning:

- Don't sign up for the executive of writers' organizations just to become known. Organizational work can encroach insidiously on your time till it has taken every spare moment, every writing moment. Unless you really love meetings, steer clear. Unless you want an excuse to give up writing, don't take the office. Unless your writing efforts are really only hot-air balloons, ration your committee work rigorously.

ALLISON SAYS:

Among the famous, and sometimes notorious, crowd pleasers was Dylan Thomas. His wonderful BBC renditions of such beautiful pieces as "Fern Hill" and "A Child's Christmas in Wales" have been replayed for generations of fans and students on both sides of the Atlantic. His American tours, on which he delighted and sometimes shocked his listeners, turned up legions of admirers.

The best Canadian speakers and readers I have heard are Robertson Davies and Alistair MacLeod.

Davies was an excellent actor who clearly enjoyed being on stage. Listening to him was fun. One would guess that a good deal of his literary success, initially anyway, stemmed from his masterful performances.

On stage, Alistair MacLeod is equally effective. When I heard him hold forth he was in Moncton, invited to participate in the Northrop Frye Literary Festival. His largest - and I would think - most difficult-to-entertain audience was a capacity crowd of high school students in the Moncton High School's large auditorium. Present at the behest of their teachers, these teenagers were not, I suspected, going to be so attentive as the mature audiences Alistair MacLeod was slated to speak to at the other festival events.

I was wrong. He is charismatic on stage, such an excellent reader and speaker that he holds his audience in thrall. Knowing by heart the first part of the story he read, he spoke the words directly to the audience, which by then was hooked. No squirming. No whispering. When he had finished reading the rest of the story, he asked for questions. There were lots of good ones. The response was terrific. Impressive.

You'll have lots of ideas on how to keep yourself in the public eye without suffering pangs of pre-appearance jitters. You could even find it fun. Never be afraid to pass on ideas to your publisher. Especially if they are not expensive – ESPECIALLY IF THEY ARE FREE – your publisher will pounce upon them with glee.

CHAPTER SEVEN:

Well, Then, How DO I Write, Anyway?

Welcome to the last chapter. You are almost ready to begin.

Chapter 7 comes in 6 parts:

A. Setting up to Write

B. Never Forget Your Reader

C. Theme, Layering, Symbolism

D. Narrators, Point of View, Voice

E. Learning Your Craft

F. Summary, Conclusions, and Oops, I Forgots!

Section A: Setting up to Write

Who Should Write?

What?

Where?

When?

And Why?

Who Should Write?

You should write.

If you have read this book to this point, you must have a yen to write.

You may have a lot to learn.

You probably do have a lot to learn - we all do - but *you* are ready to

BEGIN.

You should write

If you want to write

If you have something to say

If your delight is in the work and the finished pages, not in anticipated rewards that come with being a published author.

If you feel driven to write, you *must* write, or you will never have an hour's peace.

Write.

Don't die with your music still in you.

(Bernie Siegel)

Few reasons justify not writing if one really wants to - plenty of excuses, but no reasons. Stephen Hawking wrote *A History of Time* in his power chair, control of his body almost non-existent. Shawn Jennings wrote *Locked In Locked Out* when he had only two fingers functioning. Everyone knows about Helen Keller.

Nor is age a reason. We have already mentioned Kali Brazier-Tompkins' *A Wolf to Remember*, begun when she was eleven, finally published when she was sixteen. We have also (at DreamCatcher) read a very creditable novel by a young man of twelve and the first of a series of stories by a girl about the same age.

And as I was proofing this chapter, a box of books of various kinds, both poetry and prose, arrived in our office, sent by a teacher at work in our district. These books are all the work of local students in our schools.

Both Allison and I began to write very young. We may not have been published then, but we were writing. And I dare say we will keep on, and on, and on into the sunset. P.G. Wodehouse, after all, was at work on his last novel up to his last day on Earth at the age of 95.

Writing is a love you can begin to explore as soon as you can hold a crayon, and continue till you can't hold a crayon any longer. Begin, and placing one word after another, continue.

ALLISON SAYS:

APPRENTICESHIPS AS REPORTERS/JOURNALISTS

Apart from courses, there are other ways to serve a literary apprenticeship. One of the best-known and time-tested is reporting for a newspaper or magazine. Although for most people this is a more stressful and strenuous approach to literary composition than participating in a writing course, because of the need for haste in procuring accurate information and setting it down clearly, journalism nevertheless provides the would-be writer with considerable valuable experience in short order.

Stephen Crane, Ernest Hemingway, Gabrielle Roy and Alden Nowlan are among well-known writers who served their novitiates as reporters cum journalists.

Crane reported, from time to time, for two New York papers, the "Herald" and the "Tribune". His most famous short story, "The Open Boat", was closely based on his earlier factual account of a shipwreck off the Florida coast. The autobiographical element in this story is strong since Crane, like his fictional correspondent, was one of the survivors who made it to shore in the open boat described.

Hemingway's apprenticeship as reporter for the Toronto "Star" has been well documented, and later provided him with a lot of material for his fictional works. One can also conjecture that his travels as a correspondent in search of facts had much to do with his later international quests for fictional material.

Canadian prize-winning author Gabrielle Roy, another reporter turned novelist, began her literary career by writing for a Montreal-based agricultural magazine. One of her assignments was to return to her native Manitoba to interview and write about immigrant settlers. The success of these pieces (which were eventually collected in book form) gave her confidence as a writer and opened publishers' doors to her subsequent, famous fictional works.

Crane, Hemingway and Roy were all fortunate as jouralists in that the publications they worked for not only paid them enough to live on but covered their travel costs as well. Maritime reporter, Alden Nowlan, covering events in and around Saint John, New Brunswick, was less well off. Nevertheless, several of his most memorable and ironic poems - "In the Newsroom" and "The Execution" -

are the result of his experiences during these years.

Other aspiring writers who reported for small town newspapers were not so fortunate - nor did they have the same expectations as those who worked for urban dailies. The hundreds of weekly newpapers across this country were not, by and large, able to pay their reporters a living wage, let alone give them travel money. At least this was the case in my youth. Nevertheless, such papers provided people like myself with worthwhile experience.

The summer I turned seventeen, reporting for the local "Recorder," I learned how to meet deadlines, to research facts and get them straight - and to come to the point in as few words as possible. Unfortunately, since payment was by the word - at five cents each - I did not make enough money to contribute substantially to my upcoming first year of university.

SELF-STARTING WRITERS

In days gone by, before the proliferation of courses, seminars and writers-in-residence, aspiring writers were self-taught and often lacked formal education. They honed their skills by diligence and practise. Most of them were avid readers, their own writing tending to be at least partly a response to the literary output of others.

Alden Nowlan, a mostly self-educated man, was one of these voracious readers. During his poverty-stricken youth in Nova Scotia's Valley, Nowlan systematically worked his way through the local library's stacks. He walked substantial distances in all weathers to get these books and "he read everything," the librarian who checked out books for Nowlan told a friend of mine who lived nearby.

Once many such ardent readers begin to write in earnest, they tend to read less and less. Many find, as I have, that once they are really immersed in their own work - particularly a book - reading is a distraction they do not have much time for. This is not true for everyone, however: a Nova Scotia writer friend with whom I correspond seems to read just as much as ever when writing his books.

CHILD WRITERS

Quite a few children - as young as six, seven or eight - decide to try their hand at creative writing. Unhampered by the doubts which often assail their elders, the ones I have observed plunge in enthusiastically. In their haste to get down their story, play or poem, these youngsters often opt to spell phonetically rather than conventionally.

Because many teachers and parents regard these phonetically spelled creations with disfavor - and such pieces are certainly harder to read - their first reaction tends to be to complain about the "bad spelling" and protest that they can't read the piece in its phonetic format. This is a mistake. Often these creative efforts are entertaining and original - and well worth overcoming one's qualms about the unconventional spelling. Child writers of this age should not be subject to the rules which govern their adult counterparts.

Children who are nagged about "mistakes" in these early creative efforts tend either to stop writing these expressive pieces or to opt for a wooden style - albeit a well-spelled one - which they find is more favorably received by the adults they seek to please.

So although I am impatient with adults who turn in badly spelled manuscripts, I favor giving young children a lot of leeway. They'll have time to brush up on their spelling.

Similarly, I think little children should not be criticised for designing a cover for a book they intend to write but haven't yet begun. A surprising number of children have this urge.

When I was six or seven, I drew and colored a

cover for a book I was sure I was going to write. My mother informed me that book covers were never designed before the book was written. Devastated by this piece of information, I gave up making book covers for good and shelved my writing plans for several years.

Until I was grown up I was convinced that my childish inclination to start a book with its cover was unusual and certainly bizarre. Apparently not. All three of my children and two out of three of the youngsters I had in a kindergarten/grade 1 class quite spontaneously produced covers for books they said they intended to write. Remembering how my own early attempts of this nature had been squelched, I supported their efforts. One of these children, now grown, illustrates and designs book covers commercially and two of the others have written books.

Moving on now, closer and closer to the moment when your work must begin, pause once more and consider:
What do you want to write?

Well, that's easy.   Poetry

or

Prose

If Prose,

Fiction

or

Non-fiction

Easy. Or maybe not.

What if you want to write a poem about a tree outside your window, an account of the last years of your grandmother's life, *and* a story about this strange (imaginary) man who came to your door one night and... and something strange (imaginary) happened.

The answer to that question is: Try All Three. You'll soon find your niche.

Some people can do all things and do them well. Allison has a long list of credits: many poems, scads (her word) of short pieces both non-fiction and short stories, and book-length works of both fiction and non-fiction. If you read carefully her contributions to this book, you will find a well of clear, pure information for you to drink from.

I, on the other hand, can advise only on fiction for adults and working with publishers' editors, because that's all I know. I have written two poems in my life, each of which had to insist it was a poem before I would stop thinking of it as prose. I wrote a short story once, for one of my daughters for Christmas a year or two ago, and completely surprised her. And as for non-fiction, till I started this book I never had the slightest urge. I write novels.

Don't worry. You'll know.

ALLISON SAYS:

A GREAT IDEA!

So you're convinced you've got a great idea! The temptation is to share it with whomever is nearby - your neighbor, your best friend, your spouse.... Don't!

Try to avoid discussing what you are planning to write. If you chat at length about your proposed work, chances are you won't set your ideas down - not right away anyway. Then, when you think you are ready to put pen to paper, you may not feel so enthusiastic about what you planned to write, especially if your sounding board has not been particularly receptive.

When you have an idea which really grabs you, at least jot down the bare bones. By doing that you will probably have saved the essence of your poem, article, story or book to develop later. Hard as the uninitiated may find it to believe, even someone far too young to experience 'senior moments' is apt to lose a 'great idea' if he/she doesn't at least get down its gist - enough to jog the memory later.

Most writers or would-be writers have had the disheartening experience of losing, at least temporarily, an idea which they feel could be the basis of an enchanting piece. One former student of mine in the throes of writing her first short story told me she got so upset about thoughts related to her story getting away from her that she eventually kept pen and paper with her all the time - even by her bedside at night.

"Before I kept writing materials close by," she told me, "I lost some really good thoughts, especially at night. I was so sure I could never forget them. I sleepily convinced myself that there was no way they'd slip my mind, and that, besides, I was too tired to write them down just then. But I learned my lesson the hard way. Now, when I get flashes of insight into my character or plot, or think of an analogy which seems as if it will illuminate what I'm getting at, I hurry to get down these passing thoughts - feeling almost as driven to protect them and attend to them as I did my children when I heard them cry out in the night."

By the way, the short story this student wrote for my class turned out to be excellent - the first of many moving stories she wrote after 'graduating' from the course.

Were you surprised that Allison didn't mention losing your great idea to theft? That's because nobody is going to steal it.

It is true that occasionally a really great idea (like Darwin's *The Origin of Species*, for example) an idea whose time has come, will be reached by more than one great mind at the same time. But garden-variety ideas are perfectly safe. Other writers have plenty of their own, and will always prefer theirs to yours.

When I was teaching high school English, I used to assign the title "The Colour was Red" to each new class. "Here's the title," I would say. "Write a short story to go with it." Then I would wait with glee till the papers came in. I read stories about everything from blood, a new red dress, a red-haired boy, to Mars, the red planet.

Several years ago, Percy came to one of my seminars with a MS clutched to his chest. Literally. He was afraid to let anyone see it; we might take it from him. As far as I know, that story has never been published.

Don't do that. How many times has your car been stolen?

Poetry

Poetry doesn't sell well. You'll hear that; I say so myself. But it's not true. *Some* poetry doesn't sell. *Much* poetry doesn't sell. *But some does.*

Much poetry is written. I suspect that many more people are writing poetry than prose. Competition for publication space is therefore keen and you may end up singing your songs to an audience of none. But sing them. If they're in you, let them out.

ALLISON SAYS:

Poetry, in contrast to fiction, is often a more direct - frequently, but not always, a more subjective - reflection of the author's perceptions and feelings. Robert Frost's "The Road Not Taken" and "Tree By My Window" suggest this sort of personal revelation. Like many excellent poems, these two are brief, the imagery revealing and just right for conveying the poet's point of view. Dylan Thomas's "Fern Hill" is another wonderful poem which appears to record the poet's feelings about himself (in childhood), a place and a few moments in time. At the same time as all these poems are very individual expressions they continue to have a universal appeal.

Still, since poetry has few cut and dried rules, the poet can, and does, approach his subject from very disparate perspectives. So it is that in many successful poems the author stands back and observes other people and situations. Frost's "Death of a Hired Man" and Edwin Arlington Robinson's Tilbury Town (Gardiner, Maine) poems, many of which, such as "Mr. Flood's Party", "Richard Cory" and "Miniver Cheevy" are brief but moving and insightful character sketches.

If you have a really compelling interest, something you know a lot about and love - (gardening fits that bill for me) - it seems natural to use analogies related to it in your poetry. Mine it! The fragments of gold you pan out of your individual stake in the stream bed may gleam. One hopes that the images you conjure up from this strong personal focus will be fresh and appeal to others who find in your work a reflection of some of their own feelings - though perhaps they haven't put their perceptions into words.

For instance, a poem of mine which was most recently anthologized in 2002 (in the Nelson English series, Between The Lines 11 - a text for high schools) uses garden analogies. Called "Berrypicking", it is, however, essentially about relationships - about the qualities the protagonist hopes to find in a mate. The decisive test for her is how he performs picking berries - whether in the course of an often tedious undertaking he shows

*that he possesses such enduring qualities as pa-
tience and good temper, attributes she deems essential for a long-term relationship.*

Berrypicking

Before choosing a mate
I would need to have him
as my berrypicking companion
all one summer
from the time
of the first wild strawberries
till the cranberries and blackberries
were frost-finished

Then I would know
All about his character

Whether he persevered
despite blackflies and sunburn
Whether he picked
the berries clean
or carelessly
tore off the leaves as well

Whether he stayed
to fill the pail
or bored
by the buzzing loneliness
of field or wood

left it half-filled
and went off
to join the others
in the house

Whether he worked
with ease and pleasure
at my side
or angry
one day
that I had almost filled my pail
and he had not
pushed my hand
so that my berries
spilled upon the ground
were trampled underfoot

Should he pass
all these natural tests
of berrypicking
I would know
he was just right for me

NON-FICTION

As in poetry, the point of view of non-fiction varies. There is no hard and fast factor which determines whether the first or third person narrative is most successful.

However, when the author is describing something he has done - where his exploits and observations are the essence of the book, the account is not only going to be related in the first person, but will probably be "up close and personal." Such a book is Nova Scotian (Brier Islander) Joshua Slocum's Sailing Alone Around the World (1900). Since Slocum was not only a first-rate mariner, but a witty and to-the-point narrator, his book is well worth reading.

Slocum, of course, is only one of many successful narrators of first-hand experiences - some book length (like his) or John McPhee's much lauded West Coast account of his travels in the North, Coming Into The Country (1977); others, articles such as many in the National Geographic.

Self-help and how-to books also tend to be related from a first person point of view. This makes sense, since by and large, the reader isn't going to consider learning about raising animals or building houses from someone who hasn't had considerable success doing the thing he is discussing.

There are, however, exceptions to this generalization. Medical self-help books are frequently an accumulation of facts which the author has gleaned from various sources, and usually also rely on the writer's own experience. Similarly, books on how to bring up healthy and well-adjusted children and how to achieve successful relationships tend to be gleanings from various sources. Interestingly, authors of these books on relationships, while they may be theoretically knowledgeable about their subject, are frequently not all that successful in their own relationships.

A great many - perhaps most - non-fiction works are not first person accounts, including my own books in this category. Having made use of an accumulation of sources - archival papers, first hand-observations, interviews with appropriate people - the author stands back and writes what he or she hopes is an objective view of the chosen topic. However, as with any other subject the writer touches, he needs to know inside out what he is writing about and care deeply about how he puts together his accumulated knowledge. Such a book needs to be both accurate and readable.

Sticking to the Truth of What you are Writing:

Nobody can write about the Amazon with any authority who has not been there. I suspect that people do, but they are just using names. Events take place, ostensibly on the Amazon, but nobody is supposed to take them seriously. They could easily be happening on some other river - real or imaginary. I always advise writers not to set a story in a place where they have not lived for at least a full year.

But how much truth is true?

This problem arises when you try to write fiction based on an actual event or a life you know.

Penny came to us with a MS that she said was the story of her grandmother's life but she meant it to be a novel. Fine. Apparently there had been some very interesting periods in her grandmother's life.

But Penny felt shy about trying to enter into her grandmother's mind and heart to describe how she had felt about and reacted to the events of her life, which Penny would have to do if she were to write an effective novel. She felt that others in her family would be unhappy if she did that. She felt that she should stand back as an outside observer and report what happened

Penny had bitten off more than she could chew and her novel was not very good. She had to decide: did she really want to write a novel? The hardest part of that undertaking would be picking and choosing among significant events in her grandmother's life to make a coherent story. Or did she want to write a biography, which would allow her to include events that would have seemed important to her grandmother as she lived her life but would not contribute to the story as a novel? In other words, would she pick and choose among facts to build a coherent skeleton, then flesh it out with non-facts (fiction) to make a novel? It would it be better to write a biography, which would be as "true" as she had facts to make it?

A novel is an entity in its own right; it is not just a story.

For a beautiful example of what I mean, read Theresia M. Quigley's book *I Cry For Innocence* (DreamCatcher 2002).

I Cry describes facts and events in the author's own life, many of which happened when she was too young to remember or understand. Not an easy task for a writer. In fact, extremely taxing. I don't advise inexperienced writers to undertake it.

Before you decide to write your grandmother's story as a novel, write it as a biography; stick to the facts - no embroidery. If your family objects, don't try to publish it. Use it as a practise exercise. You'll learn technique. Then write a novel - a purely fictional account of some period in the life of some woman who might have been your grandmother. You'll learn more technique. Only then, if you still want to, try fictionalizing your grandmother's life. You may be ready by that time.

Note: Beginning writers often believe that a safe and easy way to break into the world of the published author is to write such a fictionalized biography as we have been discussing, or to write a story for children.

I hope I have now convinced you that fictionalizing facts is not at all easy. Let me assure you that neither is writing for children, neither fiction nor non-fiction. All of these forms require special techniques *in addition to* the basics needed for straight fiction or non-fiction for adult readers.

Don't worry. Pretty soon now we're going to reach the "Well, then, how in the world *do* I write?" stage.

Journals:

Especially, avoid writing to exorcize your demons, if you want to publish. Writing a journal can clarify your thinking and point to ways to solve problems, but as Julia Cameron says: "Art is therapeutic, not therapy."

That is, if writing a journal leads to a love affair with any art form, and then to a life-long commitment, great. But just because you had a terrible childhood and have written it all down doesn't mean that you have written a book that should be published.

The first readers of cathartic journals usually slobber, through tears, "Oh, honey! This is *so* sad. You are *so* brave to have written it all down. It really should be published."

That sort of first reader only builds false hopes and sets up the writer for more rejection. And hasn't she had enough of that already?

At DreamCatcher we are offered many journals. I have read a few. We have published only one and intend to publish another. One or two more, though valuable documents, were not publishable because... Remember? Publishing is business, and these journals would have done well to sell 50 copies. We advised those writers to, by all means, have a few copies printed for family, and to place a copy or two in provincial, national, or professional archives. And let it go at that.

We published Shawn Jennings's account of his brainstem stroke because Shawn Jennings was a much-loved family physician with a large practice when he suffered his stroke; his readership might, then, be large. His account of stroke from the inside out - the doctor as patient - would be valuable to the medical profession and to other stroke victims and their families everywhere. And this book was a delight to read. He was humble, un-complaining, interested in what had happened to him and its aftermath, grateful for help and love, hopeful, and funny.

I first read Shawn's MS at home. I didn't want to read it at all. I thought it would be sad and depressing. But as the day went by, sometimes I laughed so hard the dog came to see what was going on.

Shawn's book *Locked In Locked Out* was a Canadian best seller even before it had had much exposure outside the Maritimes. We think that readers will be equally interested in Janet Knudsen's *The Porcelain Doll*, which is the story of her struggle with mental illness. If you have something like those two books to offer, please come see us - or some other publisher. Otherwise, the competition is pretty keen.

My own preference is for pure fiction, even though it doesn't sell like non-fiction. When I'm writing fiction, I'm having a great time, thoroughly enjoying what I do, and not worrying at all about where the next meal is coming from. (Though I am greatly enjoying sounding off in this book.)

WRITE WHAT YOU HAVE TO SAY.

Our main point is that, whatever you want to write, *you* should do it.
that you *should* do it.
that you should *do it*.

ALLISON SAYS:

I envy writers who have a special place - sometimes even more than one - to write. Such places -
a study, a studio, a cottage on the same property,
a national or international writers' retreat where
everything is laid on - sound terrific.... Perfect....
Ideal. But unfortunately, 'escapes' like these have
not been for me.

I keep imagining how much better and more
prolific my output over the years might have been
with a private place like one of these to work. A
good many writers - several I know personally and
others I've only read about - have such tucked-
away places for either short or long-term sojourns,
sometimes both. Among the latter - writers I've read
about, that is - are John Updike, Alistair MacLeod
and Barbara Gowdy.

John Updike apparently has a series of writing rooms - one for the current novel, another for
short pieces, and still another for ... well, I can't
remember what.

Then I've heard that Alistair MacLeod has a
separate writing cottage on his Cape Breton property where he spends most summers. Besides that,
he was fortunate while at work on his masterpiece,
No Great Mischief, to be chosen for a sojourn at the

select and secluded writers' hideaway in Scotland, Hawthornden Castle. Here, I've read, the writer's days are free of the usual interruptions and distractions, even phone and fax communiqués. Only at breakfast and evening dinner, both served in the dining room, does the writer descend to converse with others. Lunch is brought up on a tray to his private and well-appointed rooms.

Barbara Gowdy lives alone in an isolated house just large enough to accommodate herself and her cat, a place with few distractions. She has been quoted as saying, "I don't know how I could get ideas or how I would know what I think about anything if I had the distraction of people in the house." She speculates too that, if she had "succumbed" to domesticity and children, she would perhaps have produced three rather than the six books she has had published so far. Yet by times - as when she was finishing her current novel, The Romantic - finding even her secluded house not sufficiently free from interruptions - she retreated to a hotel room for several weeks at a time, a place where maid service and ordered-in meals gave her absolute freedom from distractions.

Not all writers, though, need to be - or are able to be - quite so aloof from the workaday world. A writer such as Carol Shields, who early on "succumbed" to domesticity and having children - five of them - has somehow managed to find time and places (I don't know where she has written over the years or where she writes now) to turn out novels galore - many of them prize-winners.

So it seems to me that, if you are driven to write, you are going to find a time and a place - even if it's in the car while you're parked and waiting for children or a husband, at the end of the dining room table when the table is free, or at a library, where, despite stage whispers and other people moving around you from time to time, you are pretty much assured that none of these background disturbances - including the ringing of telephones - is going to need your attention.

These latter seemingly less-than-ideal locations have mostly been where I have worked - apart from the odd sojourn in a spare upstairs bedroom at my elder daughter's house, where the only household task which was my responsibility was cooking the meals. It was there I began one of my earlier books and wrote the two final short stories for my recently-completed collection, Truth to Tell: Stories from Here and Away.

Waiting indefinitely for the suitable time and propitious circumstances to put pen to paper is generally a mistake. Procrastination in writing, as in most of life's endeavors, is a bad idea. Making time - even half an hour every day - is what the would-be writer needs to do. After all, as I used to tell my students - and keep telling myself - if one were to write only a page a day one would have 365 pages at year's end.

Even most seasoned writers find they have to set themselves a time to write - and stick to their schedule as closely as possible - just as dedicated swimmers and runners mostly adhere to their daily practise periods.

INSPIRATION AND ROUTINE

Although not every one of these set-aside times is productive, the routine does pay off. Waiting for inspiration to strike is generally a mistake. Not that I don't believe in inspiration: it's just that I've found inspiration tends to come unexpectedly in the midst of a routine struggle to get down precisely what one wants to say. Inspiration is likely, I think, to be triggered in a mind focused on the subject one is striving to elucidate. As well, the serious writer's productive thoughts and feelings about this subject are often brewing while he or she is engaged in other individual pursuits which are seemingly unrelated to writing, such as gardening, preparing meals, swimming, even driving. At least I have found this to be so.

DISCIPLINE

The need for discipline foils a lot of people's writing plans. Instead of watching that extra T.V. show, lingering daily over morning coffee with friends, expending all one's early-in-the-day energy on running, bicycling or other strenuous exercise, a writer, especially an unproved wordsmith, needs to go off by herself/himself and get cracking. The socializing and exercising can come later in the day.

Not only the discipline, but the solitary nature of such a sequestered pursuit is, however, temperamentally unsuitable for many people.

But if one is serious about writing, taking the bull by the horns and making a start is crucial - advice oldtimers liked to dispense when they or someone close to them was faced with any time-consuming and demanding task. There's a lot of truth in the old adage "Only begin and the work shall be completed."

Whenever I think along these lines I remember sadly the case of a retired neighbor of my parents, a man who had lived and worked in the Orient most of his life and who stressed every time he saw me that he was about to begin a really fascinating book about his experiences abroad. He made this announcement many mornings across the garden fence over a period of six or seven years, after which he rushed off to play tennis until he was exhausted. As far as I know he never got started on what he imagined was to be his life's most significant work.

The last time I saw him he was in the early stages of Alzheimer's. He stood at my parents' back door and said, "I had something important I meant to do. Now I can't remember what it was. That makes me sad."

Listening to this pathetic confession, I myself felt close to tears.

UNAVOIDABLE INTERRUPTIONS

There are, of course, as I mentioned earlier, unavoidable interruptions to one's ideal schedule. Chief among these are commitments to family and job. Extended illness is right up there too.

Putting children and a spouse off when they need you is a bad idea, though they should be cautioned not to interrupt you on an idle whim. If one can, it is best to find a time when everyone else in the household is out, asleep or otherwise occupied.

Also, if you have to earn a living while you are discovering whether writing is what you want to do full time and whether it will pay off sufficiently in dollars and cents to support your lifestyle, you will find yourself obliged first of all to fulfill your workaday obligations faithfully. With these obligations, finding time to write is difficult.

Because of my own family-first policy - which included lots of good meals at reasonable hours, time for games and help with homework - and because I held a demanding job, my writing time while the children were young was limited to an hour or so after their early bed times. It was then, usually after I'd had a bath and crawled into bed myself, that I wrote most of my early poems. (This evening hour is no longer a good writing time for me. These days, once most of the day is spent, my energy level for creative endeavors is depleted. Fortunately, I am now able to write most mornings - always my best time. Thus it happens that for people like me writing times change over the years, altered to keep pace with changing lifestyles.)

Because of so many obligations at home and work during my twenties and early thirties, I wrote poems (quite a number of them), articles (a lot of these too) and a few stories. The books had to come later, though, interestingly enough, six or seven of my initial books grew out of the short pieces I had written early on.

Section B: Readers
Never Forget Your Reader

As you write, never forget your reader.

The rest of this chapter is based on notes for a seminar for writers of fiction that I gave May 26 and 27, 2000. Much of it will also help writers of non-fiction.

Introduction

The Four Functions of Authors:

1. Know that you want to write for *your Reader*, and never forget *your Reader*.
2. Know what *your themes* are, and be conscious of which of your themes you are using in the MS you are working on today.
3. Choose the best *narrator* for each story. Then clear out of the way and let the story come through the narrator.
4. *Master your craft.*

An author is a storyteller craftsman.

Note: The he/she/they problem: I don't want to be forever saying "he or she," and I absolutely reject this business of "they" when I mean "he or she." I will therefore alternate. In the first section I will use "he," in the second, "she." In this way I hope to avoid clumsiness, and "political offensiveness" as well. You will know that I mean everybody.

The most common error of beginning writers, in my experience, is *Forgetting the Reader*.

And so, everything I tell you in these notes is geared toward keeping *your Reader* with you.

Whether you are writing fiction or non-fiction; poetry, science, or a formal essay, in effect you are telling a story. You tell; the Reader listens.

But as a writer you have a special problem: How do you know whether your Reader is listening or gone down to the pub?

Well, suppose you hung out with a bunch of friends and told each other stories. What would happen?

Answer: Constant feedback.

Suppose you read stories to each other.

Again: Constant feedback.

Now suppose your stories appeared in a magazine without anyone seeing them in advance.

Ah! No feedback, at least not when you needed it.

RULE: **A writer has constantly to assess what the feedback from the Reader would probably be, and if necessary, to adjust his work to ensure that the feedback will be what the writer wants: tears, fury, interest... whatever reaction the work is designed to evoke.**

Any reaction may be called for. Make sure you understand what your MS wants. If you don't get it right… well, you've laughed at passionate love scenes, perhaps? Exactly.

In these notes, as examples, I cite several good novels, and one or two not so good; also a short story and a poem. Here's the first:

Bellwether by Connie Willis, a contemporary American writer.

Bellwether evokes irritation – a rare requirement. But this story works very well, so well that it's a prize-winner.

Note: **You will be able to extend this book and turn your investment in it into profit, if you find, read, and ponder the example books Allison and I suggest. You may even want to buy some of them.**

We're talking about assessing reader reaction. That's hard to do. But there are some tricks you can use; they'll turn up as we proceed. Here's the first one:

Whenever (and wherever) you write, imagine that your Reader is with you.

In this way you define:

- who your Reader is

- how much you have to explain to that Reader – knowing your Reader includes knowing pretty much what he already knows.

- how you can keep your Reader's interest.

Then let's look at these points:

Who is your Reader?

You have to decide who your Reader is. But you don't draw this information out of the air; the MS tells you.

For example, half the novels published today are romances that offer an hour or two of escape to tired, bored, disillusioned women.

Once you have identified your Reader

- picture your *typical* Reader

- find pictures of him (more likely, her)

- pin up your pictures so you can see them as you write

- put little signs saying "Reader" on your monitor, on the back of your left hand, on your coffee cup – for a while, till remembering your Reader becomes automatic.

How much will you have to explain to your Reader?

Your Reader is probably someone who might have been with you when you experienced the raw material for your MS.

RULE: Write about what you know.

Perhaps you were in the army, or were working in a hospital when a disaster occurred, or grew up listening to the Beatles, or Celine Dion... You see? Lots of people can identify with your thought – a whole raft of readers ready-made.

Once you have sorted out who your Reader is, you know how much of the background of your story he already knows. So...

RULE: Be specific about your Reader for everything you write, and write for him.

What will keep your Reader with you?

I'll tell you what that is:

- lively writing that moves right along

    in fiction:

    - lots going on

    - characters doing things and talking

    - appeals to emotions

- and the exact amount of information your Reader needs to stay with you.

Let's look at the last of these requirements: Give your Reader the *exact* amount of information he needs. Not more. Not less. (Now do you see the need for a *specific typical* Reader?)

RULE: **Resist every temptation to lecture, preach, or teach.**

Readers won't be talked down to. Editors won't accept it. And publishers won't publish it.

If you know that you feel urged to lecture, preach, or teach, write this rule in Christmas lights and keep it flashing all year long:

Do not lecture, preach, or teach.

The only information the Reader needs or wants from *you* is:

In non-fiction:
- information/description/facts pertinent to the subject

In fiction:
- what the "set" of a scene is like
- where the character *of the moment is at all times*
- which character is speaking

THAT'S ALL!! The story will do the rest.

About "Sets":

Question: How much detail does the Reader need?

Answer: Very little.

Years ago I saw a movie about space travel that engaged my imagination at the time. All I can remember of it now is one scene – really just the set for the scene. Two people were in a small control room in which everything was beige: walls, consoles, chairs, uniforms, even the hair and skin of the two crew members who were there. But there was one Granny Smith apple in that room. That's what I mean. (In case you're wondering, Granny Smiths are bright green.)

The Reader will fill in the corners of your picture. You need supply only the main points, those the Reader *must* notice if he is not to miss something important.

If, for example, a scene takes place in a kitchen where the characters are sitting at a table eating breakfast, you supply

- the table – size, material of manufacture, condition, whatever is relevant, but *only* what is relevant

- the food – what they are eating, if it tastes good, if it's plentiful or scanty – only what is relevant.

Your Reader will fill in the rest, even to the dishes.

All you need do is provide colour. That is, local colour, colour commentary – that colour.

To do this, let the characters feel textures, see colours, smell aromas, taste flavours, and hear the tones of the voices as the characters speak to each other.

But do this with nouns and verbs.

Eschew adverbs and adjectives, or you'll commit the sin of overwriting. Bad! Very bad!

And make sure that your Reader will experience these sensations too. No Reader wants to be told; he wants to take part. Remember: **No lecturing, preaching or teaching.** Remember that!

As illustration:

Joni leaned on the table with both elbows, holding her coffee mug between her hands. That wonderful smell of fresh-brewed coffee filled the air she breathed, and she smiled.

Do you see what happened here? The narrator allowed Joni, the character, to experience the table, the mug, the coffee aroma. The narrator was inside Joni's experience, so the Reader was there too. Narrator gave Reader what she wanted: vicarious experience. When we discuss beginnings, we will speak again about reaching out of a story and drawing a reader in. Here we have an example of what that feat involves.

I would lose my Reader if I wrote, for example:

Joni, who was leaning with both elbows on the old kitchen table, held a chipped blue coffee mug that said "Souvenir of Calais" on the side, in her hand. The steam from the cup rose into her nostrils. She smiled.

This second version is

- overloaded with detail.

- Joni is separated from her smile by so much information they never join up – the Reader is not sure why she smiled.

- But most importantly – this version is not experienced, it is reported. The Reader senses a heavy-handed, boring narrator in the background and runs for cover. For you, the writer, this is real bad news!

Note: When we came to this sentence during the seminar, off the top of my head I said, "You should be able to begin with this sentence and write a novel." Afterward, I thought, *I wonder if they could.* I found out. They could. Because I did. Something like 80,000 words later I had written a humorous romance called *Blackberry Light*, which begins with Joni sitting at her new glass-topped table in her new A-frame cottage, looking out at Dipper Harbour early on a sunny June morning. She is drinking coffee and smiling.

Note: I hope you can see how this beginning reaches out from inside the story, grabs hold of the reader, and yanks her in:

- Joni leans on the table with both elbows. Reader knows what that is like; she has done it loads of times.

- Joni is holding a coffee mug in her hands. Reader has done that - loads of times. It's a hot mug because the coffee is fresh-brewed, still aromatic.

- The aroma fills the air Joni breathes - not just any old air in the house, most of which is free to float around the rooms and escape out the windows, but *the air she breathes*, the air that passes through her nose and into her lungs and makes her smile. This air is incorporated into Joni's body consciously; she knows what is happening; it pleases her; she smiles.

In the novel I added a few more details to transport the unsuspecting reader into Joni's body and trap her there for the duration. Joni's feet are bare, the floor is paved with rough terra cotta tiles, her bare feet press against the tiles because she is perched on the edge of a packing case. Reader can feel it all as Joni does: the pressure on her feet as they press against the tiles, the tension in her thighs and back, that take the strain of perching on the edge of the packing case. The sharp edge of the packing case that causes these tensions. Reader is now identified with protagonist; reader *is* Joni. Reader is hooked. Keep up that kind of writing and reader will finish the book.

Here's how the novel *Blackberry Lights* begins:

June was "bustin' out all over."

June was bustin' out in northern sunshine and the pearly glow of early morning by the sea. It was bustin' out of the thin soil of Hamilton Harbour as tough little wild roses, and as lupin volunteering in gravelly patches as if by squatters' rights. It was bustin' out in Joni Plenghorn's A-frame cottage - threatening to bust right through the roof. And June was bustin' out in Joni Plenghorn's heart.

Joni perched on the edge of a packing case and leaned on her new glass-topped table with both elbows, a mug of fresh-brewed coffee in her hands. Her bare toes pressed against her terra cotta floor, feeling the tiles warm and rough and earthy. Her knees and thighs received the same solid pressure, and exulted in it. Through soft old denim the packing case cut into her botton, but her spine and shoulders met the need with pleasure, and the back of her neck felt the push of the floor as if it had been the lift in her heart. Coffee aroma filled the air she breathed, and she smiled, a slow, supremely happy smile from deep inside her soul.

Here, then, are some rules, all based on the most important among them:

RULE: NEVER BORE YOUR READER

Watch it! You may not know you're boring, but editors will. You'll never bore a Reader because you'll never reach a Reader.

Readers want to enter a story-life for a few minutes in exchange for their own, so

RULE: Let your characters "do" the story.

RULE: You keep out of your stories. Nobody wants you.

RULE: Do not stick in intrusions by the narrator.

I by N: Much more later about intrusions by the narrator, but get rid of them. You have to be very, very good before you can risk them.

Find the I by N in this little story:

"Well, here it is," John said. "Fundy shore. The place I've been telling you about for the past six months."

Janet smiled. "The place you couldn't wait to come home to," she teased. "The bay that has the highest tides in the world."

Actually, it is now known that some inlet on the coast of Ungava has tides that, for all practical purposes, are just as high.

"That's right," John replied. "The tide is away out now. Just wait till you see what happens as it comes in."

Looking for I by N's is like playing that kindergarten game of "which thing in this picture is different from all the others?"

Learn to play that game when you read over what you have written, and get rid of the odd items; remember, oddman, out.

Often I by N's come from a writer's just not being able to resist showing off a little. Don't!

Again, repeat after me:

RULE: **No lecturing, preaching, or teaching!**
     Or asides. Or smart remarks.   Or a whole lot of other stuff.
     Get rid of them. Out!!!

Here's one aspect of what I mean when I tell you to keep yourself out of sight:

Not long ago I read *Murder in Monte Carlo* by E. Phillips Oppenheim. Ever heard of him? Probably not. Yet he was as popular in the 1920's and 30's as Stephen King is now. He told a good story, but he was a technician, nothing more, and not a very good one at that.

Well, I'm reading along. A murder has occurred, and two of the main characters are dining in a Monte Carlo restaurant discussing the circumstances. I am all agog – or at least agog – to hear what they have to say. So what does Oppenheim do? He stops. He describes the restaurant and the two men in detail. (Oppenheim was an expert on Monte Carlo.) Eventually he returns to their table. Then he tells me to wait some more because they can't talk about the murder till the waiter leaves.

"Aw, come on!" says I. "Get on with it!"

Oppenheim begins again. Half a page on, somebody comes by who knows one of the characters, and we have to stop and be civil. Half a page more, somebody waves from across the room; we wave back. Three quarters of a page, and the waiter returns.

Realism, you say? But I don't want *that* realism; I want the murder. I am beginning to be irritated, and irritation is *not* what Oppenheim wants me to feel. Connie Willis, in *Bellwether*, wanted me to be irritated; Oppenheim wants me to hang on his every word till the mystery is solved. Well, I have news for you, E.P. Not every word of yours is up to my weight.

- If you stay back

- If you don't ask yourself, What should *I* be doing now

- If you let the story tell itself

- Above all, if you subordinate self to purpose, you won't be an E. Phillips Oppenheim. You'll be a better writer.

About where your characters are:

When writing scenes, put in just enough detail to allow your Reader to know *at all times* when a character he needs to follow has moved from one position to another. Not a detail more. Just enough – like follow the puck and the player who has it; don't try to keep track of the whole rink all at once and all the time.

For example:

Mary is sitting by the kitchen window in a two-story house. She can't see the stairs. Joe calls from the head of the stairs, "Mary, where's my..?" As she answers, Mary sees that Joe has a single sock in his hand.

No, no, no. She can't do that. You haven't moved her, and your Reader will be confused. You have to make Mary rise and move to the bottom of the stairs. But no more. And in the fewest possible words. Don't describe the whole house – unless you have a good reason to do so. Just get her there.

And finally,

About which character is speaking:

About the "he saids" and "she saids," more later. This simple rule now:

RULE: Use conversational tags only when your Reader won't be sure who is speaking if you don't.

If you're not sure, ask somebody to read the passage and tell you.

On this point: First Readers:

Let them read your MSS if you're comfortable doing so, but ask specific questions:

Did you know where Tom was? Were you sure who was talking on this page?

If you don't, they'll tell you either, "This is wonderful. I love it!" or "If I were you, I'd make the main character a man, not a woman; I'd set the story in New York, not Saint John; and I'd make the taxi driver on page ten speak French."

To sum up here:

One day when Brad Janes and I were working on his novel *Overtime*, I said to him:

Think of it this way. Your little daughter will soon be walking. One of these days you'll take her hand and lead her out to the street. What will you tell her? Just what she needs to know. Just "No, no, babe. We don't eat rocks." Just, "Hold tight to my hand." You won't overload her with information; you'll give her exactly what she needs – no more, no less.

In summary, the Common Errors we have touched on here (on keeping a light but firm grip on your Reader's hand) are:

1.   **Error**: Forgetting constantly to assess what feedback from the Reader is likely to be.

        Remedy: Practice, practice, practice. *And read to find out how other writers keep evoking the reactions they want.*

2.   **Error**: Lecturing, preaching, teaching. Saying to your Reader, in effect, "Now you have to understand that…"

     Remedy: Let the narrator tell the story *through the characters*. You keep your oar out of this stream.

3.   **Error**: Putting in too much description.

     Remedy: Describe only in sketches. Dwell only on essential details. Your Reader will fill in the rest.

4.   **Error**: Forgetting to move the characters on the stage of the story.

     Remedy: Be a stage director. Remember that you know far more than you're writing down, *but your Reader does not*.

5.   **Error**: Putting in too many or too few "he saids" and "she saids."

     Remedy: Ask for help.

Section C: Theme   Layering   Symbolism

Everyone wants to be daring, creative, and original. Everyone wants to do things in new ways. But unless we return over and over again to the basics, we will have no chance to truly soar.

Deng Ming-Dao
365 TAO

**Sections C, D, and E present the BASICS.
Pay strict attention**

Theme, Layering, Symbolism

We'll take these three together because they are three aspects of story-telling that are never – well, hardly ever – pointed out to the Reader.

Theme:

Another of the most common errors of beginning writers, to my mind, is ignorance of, or disregard of, the importance of theme.

Theme is the reason for, or point of, your narrative.

State your theme in one sentence and in abstract, general, non-particular terms – but only for your own use, not for the Reader's eyes.

Do this as soon as your theme is clear to you, and never stray from it. Your story will run out of control if you stray, and you'll lose your Reader.

In *Pride and Prejudice* Jane Austen stated her theme as the opening sentence:

"It is a truth universally acknowledged, that a single man in possession of a good fortune must be in want of a wife."

And she never strayed from that proposition, and stopped only when all the young men of good fortune had been fixed up.

Nowadays we don't usually state our themes so baldly, but every well-made story has one; and you should be able to find your theme anywhere in your novel, as you can find blood in every part of your body.

Then what are your themes?

Well, what do you love, hate, or fear, with a passion? (Ray Bradbury)

There you find your themes.

Mark Twain loved the Mississippi. That love still glows in everything he wrote about the river, and *Tom Sawyer* and *Huckleberry Finn* are perhaps the best American novels to this day.

Dickens hated injustice. That emotion comes through every cruel stepfather, every hopeless crossing sweeper, every slum tenement he wrote about. Try reading one of his, perhaps *Nicholas Nickelby* or *Bleak House* or *David Copperfield*.

It's easier to see the themes of the old masters, who have left us a finished body of work that can be studied, than to see the themes of today's writers; but we can take a stab at some of them. I think one of Janet Turner Hospital's themes may be fear of the cult mentality, mental slavery. Try her novel *Oyster*.

Ray Bradbury says that themes are

"…truths of explosive self-revelation and continuous astonishment at what your deep well contains if you just haul off and shout down it."

Zen in the Art of Writing
I highly recommend this book

Bradbury seems to like explosions. Explosions of many kinds occur in his stories, and he says of himself in *Zen*, "Every morning I jump out of bed and step on a landmine. The landmine is me. After the explosion, I spend the rest of the day putting the pieces together. [And he adds] Now it's your turn. Jump!"

Bradbury is a wonderful guide for writers. He'll tell you that these wells he speaks of don't run dry. You can always shout down them and scare up something you love, or hate, or fear.

That is, **there is no such thing as writer's block.**

I'll repeat that:

THERE IS NO SUCH THING AS WRITER'S BLOCK

There are procrastination, excuses, broken fingers... but there is no such thing as writer's block.

So when you have discovered your themes,

- welcome them
- don't be afraid of them
- look them in the eye and dramatize them
- and start pouring them on paper. (Bradbury)

You can find a few minutes every single day to write.

The night Julia Cameron's daughter was born, Julia sat up writing about what was happening till she had to wake her husband and tell him, "It's time." (*The Right to Write*)

What about the *"with a passion"* part?

Well, for writers there's national or community passion and individual passion.

The Irish, for example, have produced a wonderful literature for years out of their national tragedies. The African-Americans, from Phillis Wheatley, the first of their writers, herself a slave, to Toni Morrison and Maya Angelou, have written about the suffering of their people, with a passion. Canadians, except for the people of Quebec, don't have a national passion (apart, a lot of people would say, from hockey!!); you will have to settle for your individual ones.

But make sure you use your own passions, not borrowed ones, not simply popular ones – like the dysfunctional family for its own sake - or ones that you think will sell. You'll bore yourself before you ever threaten to bore a Reader.

Your theme + your style = originality. (More about style and originality later.)

You now know, then, that
- your themes are already in you
- they are all ready to appear as MSS.

Note: Notice "already" and "all ready."

Yes, if you're a writer, themes turn into MSS. If you're a writer, that's what you do with themes. If you're a painter, you make pictures of them. If you're a baker, you make bread. A milliner, you make hats.

Some say fiction has only three themes:

love

money

politics

Note: A story may have elements of one, or two, or all three, but a good story always has a theme. If a story rambles, it may lack a theme; if it has no theme, it will ramble.

RULE: **Know your theme and stick to it.**

If true, is this small number of themes a problem?

No. Your themes may be the same as half the town's, but others won't write your stories, and you won't write theirs.

As an illustration:

The Old Man and the Sea
Hemingway

What would you say "The Old Man…" is about?

"Well, it's about this old man…"

No. That's character, not theme.

"Well, then, it's about catching this big fish…"

Uh-uh. That's plot.

"So it's about going out on the ocean and…"

Nope. Setting.

"So all right. What *is* "The Old Man…" about?"

How about this for a definition?

> *The Old Man and the Sea* is about pitting human heart and skill, faith and dreams, against whatever the world can put up against them.

That's close. That's theme.

You may use any theme you like. You may use that one. Use it often. You won't write "The Old Man…"

"Why not?"

Well, not because you're not in Hemingway's league.
Not because it has already been done.

Because you don't know what Hemingway knew; you haven't his experiences, memories, interests… **You have yours.**

Hemingway told the story his way because he was Papa Hemingway; for no other reason. **You'll tell yours.**

Now to some Common Errors around theme:

1.   **Error**: Not being conscious of your theme.

   Remedy: Know that you have a theme, and take the trouble to define it when you begin each story.

2.   **Error**: Looking for a theme outside in the world, not inside your own mind and heart.

   Remedy: Shout down your own well.

3.   **Error**: Changing themes mid-story.

   Remedy: If your theme isn't working, don't try to salvage the story; scrap what you've done and begin again.

4.   **Error**: Wandering all around your theme.

   Remedy: Stick to it!

5.   **Error**: Trying to force a story to fit a theme not its own. Or, conversely, trying to elaborate/develop a theme with a story about something else.

   Remedy: Let each story write itself. That is, tread lightly and keep your creative genius free.

6.   **Error**: Being reluctant to cut anything and everything that doesn't have to do with your theme.

   Remedy: When writing your first draft, take down everything that comes gushing out of your head and heart; but when you revise, cut ruthlessly everything that wanders from your theme.

7.   **Error**: Explaining or stating theme.

   Remedy: Don't do it.

Layering

Layering is one of the techniques of story-telling that you don't set out to do but that you may – or may not – achieve to good effect; and your Reader may never be conscious of your story's layers.

Example 1:

Jeremy Taylor, *Amanda's Adventures*, unpublished, from Vol 3, the story of "Schrodinger's Cat."

Schrodinger was a German physicist, winner of the Nobel Prize in 1933 for work on Quantum Theory.

In March of the year 2000, this story was on the program of the meeting of the Eclectic Reading Club, read aloud by Dr. Derek Hamilton.

The members of Eclectic and their guests were delighted with "Schrodinger's Cat." Everyone laughed and smiled. Nearly everyone understood some of the satiric levels under the silly surface. Only a few, though, saw through the depths of the story. You could tell by the solitary guffaws that greeted some of Jeremy's passages from two or three places in the room, that only perhaps three of the approximately seventy people there saw down to his basic level, his theme.

Example 2:

Connie Willis, *Doomsday Book*

You have already heard of Connie Willis's book *Bellwether*, and you'll hear of it again. But *Doomsday Book*... five stars of five!

Note: Willis's. Correct present-day method for forming
the possessive of singular words ending in "s."

I want to tell you about the layers in *Doomsday Book*.

Surface: Young woman, student-historian at Oxford about a hundred years from now, goes back to Oxford in the fourteenth century and arrives as the Black death reaches the town. At the same time a killer flu virus arrives in the Oxford of her own time.

Deeper: A story about how people face adversity, such as pandemic disease, illustrated by "Surface" above.

Deeper still: An exposition of the proposition that human nature doesn't change, at least over centuries, illustrated by "Surface" and "Deeper" above.

Again Deeper: A story of courage, faith, and the nobility that "little" people sometimes display, illustrated by all of the above.

If I were you, I'd rush right out for *Doomsday Book*. But if you need something shorter, try "The Secret Sharer," a short story by Joseph Conrad. I once counted seven layers in that.

My point is that the deeper you go through the layers of a story, the closer you come to the underlying theme, and the clearer you see, that story/plot is an ephemeral vehicle for illustrating theme.

So pause when you're panting to keep up with Jack and Jill as they climb their hill (Bradbury) and give thought for a moment to what is going on deep in your "well" that is gushing out this froth you are turning into words on paper.

And a follow-up point: Becoming conscious of the layers in a story does not detract from the Reader's enjoyment. But never point them out; let your Reader find them for herself.

Now to sum up, **The Common Errors**:

1.   **Error**: Not knowing about layering, which is like setting out to make a wedding cake without knowing that nobody bakes a thing that looks like a fairy-tale palace all in one piece.

      Remedy: Open your mind/thought to the idea that your story possibly can be read on more than one level.

2.   **Error**: Thinking that layering must be done consciously and that *you* can't do it. It's not, and you can – the theme will take care of the layers.

      Remedy: Relax and let your story gush naturally from your cerebral arteries.

      Bradbury says: "Relax… into originality." (*Zen*)

3.   **Error**: Supposing that, since you want to write genre – detective stories, westerns, romances… that you don't need to know about such things. Wrong! Connie Willis has a stack of Hugo's and other honours, for *Science Fiction*.

      Remedy: Aim High.

Symbolism

You know what symbols are. You look at them and think something else – a plain gold ring, third finger, left hand, for example.

Symbols run through your story. Usually you don't choose them, they just come. If they don't come, fine, don't worry; symbols should never be forced or superimposed – put in afterwards.

Unless you make a point of looking for them, you may not know they're there, in stories by others or in your own.

When I wrote *Red Dragon Square*, I knew about some of the symbols – Johnny's gold medallion, for instance. But I didn't see the most important one, the running water symbol, till the work was finished.

When I read *Bellwether*, I thoroughly enjoyed the book, but I didn't really "see" the herd of sheep till later. Read it and you'll see what Connie Willis is saying under the irritating story-surface – and how she's doing it.

We could go on and on. In *Middlemarch* (George Eliot) an avenue of lime trees is symbolic of an outward-looking, hopeful young wife; and a yew alley symbolizes her defeated, inward-looking older husband. I pointed that out to my professor and was shamelessly proud of myself; he hadn't seen it.

Pride and Prejudice is full of status symbols.

And some books are symbolic in themselves: *The Old Man and the Sea* and *Red Dragon Square* for two.

And now to the **Common Errors** and their remedies:

1.   **Error**: Total ignorance of symbolism.

        Remedy: Simply open your eyes.

2.   **Error**: Fear of handling symbols.

        Remedy: Relax and they'll take care of themselves. Never force them or point them out.

3.   **Error**: Fear that your Reader will think you're putting on airs.

        Remedy: Relax. Ten to one she'll never notice. And one to ten she'll tell you you write great stories.

Section D: Narrator   Point of View   Voice

Learning to write novels is like learning to drive, or fly, bake, or perform any hands-on operation.

First comes the desire to do it. In novel writing, the desire is to communicate, through stories, with receptive minds – our Readers.

Then comes the theory: the why's and wherefore's of the operation we are undertaking: in novels, theme and its associated concepts.

Then finally we begin to practise our craft. We choose the narrator, establish the narrator's point of view, and begin to write.

Narrators come in

- First Person
- Third Person
- Omniscient varieties

and in

- Internal
- External types.

And first and foremost - brace yourself - **narrators control the telling of the story. *You, the author, do not.***

You can think of setting up to write a novel as setting up to produce a play. The author writes the play but has less and less to do with it as rehearsal progresses; the director takes over and puts the actors through their paces. Finally, on opening night, the author has nothing to do but take a bow, and the director has nothing much to do but pace nervously; the actors have taken over.

In making a novel you are the author, but your director (called narrator) takes over your story and pushes your actors (called characters) into line until the work is finished, when you can both go fishing.

You have readers, it's true, but most of them will notice only the characters (the stars of your show.) Only those who know your style will recognize you, and you may as well send your narrator to a monastery for all the notice he'll receive.

In the meantime, however, while the writing is going on, the narrator is king – more than that, absolute monarch – so we had better learn a little about him and his tribe.

Narrators are very simple:

First person narrators tell *I* stories:

> I went to the beach on my birthday and had a lovely time.

Third person narrators tell he/she/they stories.

> They went to the beach on her birthday…

Omniscient narrators tell "God" stories, and you are never to use one, so we'll dispose of them first.

Omniscient narrators live in every character's mind and heart and body; they see all, know all, feel all.

Run for your life! Beginning novelists sometimes think the omniscient way would be great – no limitations, no boundaries. No, no. Don't try it. You'd be mired in no time.

Very few writers have ever used this technique successfully, and even the great Henry James, who was good at it, is not read much any more, except by serious students of literature, and then more for his notes on writing than for his novels themselves. Christopher Morley said Henry James had a rush of words to the head.

No, no. You're stuck with first and third.

A note here before we go on to discover what these first and third person narrators do.

Note: Should you at any time have trouble with a story;
              should you find that it won't come together and
              flow, try changing the person of your narrator.

In one of its many drafts, *Red Dragon Square* was in third person. That didn't work. I tried first person. That worked – eventually – but I learned that you have to have the right person (character) to be narrator. The first time, I chose Johnny as the *I*, but he was wrong for the part even though he's really the main character. Then I tried Arnold and had no more trouble; the story was happy and wrote itself smooth as jelly babies.

Now then, **First Person Narrators**

First person narrators are always internal because

>*I* always know what is going on in *me*, but I can't know what goes on in other people unless they tell me.

You already know that; now think about it. Any *I* is very limited. I can know what you say and do but not what you think and feel unless you tell me. I can guess from body language and tone of voice, but I can't be sure.

First person narrators are limited in exactly the same way. They are always internal, restricted to seeing everything through the main character, and for this reason some writers think they are harder to write than third person narratives.

Compare these two little stories:

I was having a fight with Kelly. She picked on me all day, so I hit her. When I did that, Kelly got mad and hated me even more.

Grade 3 level maybe? The writer assumes what she can't really know.

And this version:

I was having a fight with Kelly. She picked on me all day, so I hit her. Then her face got red, and she yelled at me, "I hate you. I hate you even more."

This one we can deal with; the writer reports only what she can know.

You have a choice of narrators – or it seems that you do; but like a great deal more in the practice of this craft of writing fiction, the choice of narrator is often dictated by the story.

Some stories demand the first person narrator because the Reader wants to experience the action first hand. *Robinson Crusoe*, for instance, wouldn't work in third person. The Reader wants to know what it's like to be castaway on a desert island; wants to experience the adventure first hand, not to hear some third-hand report of it.

Don't worry. Relax. First person narrators aren't hard. Accept their limitations and go for it.

Third Person Narrators

The third person narrator is

- more common than first
- more flexible, therefore not so limited
- can be internal, external, or both

but faces its own limitations and dangers.

The third person external narrator:

The third person external narrator stays with the characters, follows them around, reports their activities; but the characters do not see him, nor can he know *for sure* what they are thinking or feeling. Journalists use the external narrator because of the detachment, but good novels usually demand a narrator who is right in there up to his elbows, a part of the story.

Illustration:

Ted walked down the street smiling and swinging his briefcase *as if* he thought the flowers were about to bloom in King Square, though it was still March, and cold.

That's as close as the third person *purely external* narrator can come to Ted. *He looks as if he thought...*

The third person **internal** narrator:

The third person *purely internal* narrator enters the main character and never leaves. Therefore, though he never speaks of *I* but always calls himself *Ted* or *he* (in our illustration) he is as limited as the first person fellow.

Ted walked down the street smiling and swinging his briefcase, *thinking the flowers were about to bloom*, etc.

But you can't then say,

Mary came along *thinking the flowers were about to bloom, too.*

No. Mary has to look *as if* she's thinking that. Otherwise you're getting into omniscient narrator, sliding point of view, or both.

Because of these limitations, many writers use a combination internal/external third person narrator – *never in first person, though, just third*; remember that.

Third person **combination internal/external narrator:**

The combination third person narrator is sometimes the main character; sometimes sitting up in a corner observing but unobserved, or following the characters down the street – whatever they are doing.

You are much freer with this narrator. You can choose when to go inside and when to stay out. You can choose how deep you want to go into your character's thoughts and feelings. And you can, with care, choose to enter more than one mind.

You will probably choose the combination third person narrator; but be warned, dangers lurk. We will come to them next under the heading, Point of View.

Point of View

While talking about narrators and their limitations we have been coming to Point of View.

RULE: All narrators must stick to their Point of View.

This is very Important.

Point of View is *whose head, if any, the narrator is in.*

POV problems are legion. I meet them all the time. *Please* learn what they are and correct yours.

I must stress the importance of POV.

If you aim for any degree of quality at all in your work, you must learn the POV rules and obey them.

The Rules of POV:

RULE 1:   **Stick to the limitations placed on your narrator.**

RULE 2:   **Know who your POV characters are and NEVER enter the head of any other character.**

RULE 3:   **Make only main characters POV characters, and change from one to another only at major breaks in your story – at new chapters or at major changes within chapters.**

RULE 4:   **Avoid Sliding Point of View.**

In Briann Stuart's romance novel *Double Takeout* (unpublished) she uses three POV characters: Lindsay, the female lead; Rob, her boyfriend; and Amanda, her nine-year-old daughter.

Some chapters are written from Lindsay's POV. In them the narrator enters Lindsay's head and knows what she thinks and feels, *but cannot know what the others think or feel.*

Some chapters are from Rob's POV, but *notice that we are talking about whole chapters*; the narrator never hops from one head to another within chapters.

Even in intimate scenes, if it's Lindsay's POV chapter, the Reader finds out what Rob is feeling only as he acts and speaks and Lindsay reacts to him. If it's Rob's chapter, the POV reverses, and he has to judge what Lindsay feels by her reactions.

Occasionally neither Lindsay nor Rob is available to carry the story; then the POV switches to Amanda for awhile.

When none of the three POV characters is around, the narrator becomes purely external and tells the story from outside, even if other characters are available. And, of course, even when one or more of the POV characters are present, the narrator sometimes remains external.

It seems complicated, but it's really not very hard.

Sliding Point of View

Avoid it. That is, never hop from head to head within scenes. Your Reader will think she's watching a tennis match.

But, you'll tell me, so-and-so does it all the time. So she does. Is she a good writer?

You can get away with a little sliding – very little – and still do good work. You can get away with a small I by N (Intrusion by Narrator) from time to time – a very small one. I wouldn't touch the little ones I find in Briann Stuart's work. But know what you are doing.

What Briann does I call stroking the chicken's feathers. I tell writers

You can get away with stroking the feathers now and then, but don't wring the chicken's neck.

Common Errors around narrators and their POV then:

1.   **Error**: Not knowing about narrators, what they do, and the limitations on their work.
        Remedy: Study these notes; read other novelists for technique, not just for content; and follow the rules.

2.   **Error**: Allowing intrusions by the narrator.
        Remedy: Keep yourself and your narrator out of sight. Let the characters tell the story.

3.   **Error**: Having the wrong narrator.
        Remedy: Choose carefully the first time, but if necessary, change your narrator and start again. Never simply switch narrators and carry on; you'd ruin your story.

4.   **Error**: Confusing the reader with narrator changes.
        Remedy: Be very careful of POV.

5.   **Error**: Having too many POV characters.
        Remedy: Allow POV to only a few most important characters, and then only with third person narratives.

6.   **Error**: Sliding POV.
        Remedy: *Never* head hop.

Voice

Following on from Narrators and POV, we have to consider the term Voice.

I sometimes come up against confusion over Voice.

There's Narrative Voice, which is what we have been discussing in the Narrator and POV sections.

Then there's the idea of the voice of the main character/narrator – who he/she is specifically.

This distinction is so confused and confusing that I am having trouble explaining the confusion. That's because there really isn't a distinction at all.

You will hear people speak of the voice of your characters as
The narrator speaks with the voice of the young, black, urban male in New York
or: The author's command of the voice of the disgruntled housewife is exact and sure.

There is no real distinction. Voice is voice.

Just be aware. Then you won't be confused and I won't have to confuse you further.

Voice is whom you represent:

As I recall some of the novels I am editing or have edited, I find the voices of

- a lonely, disillusioned pro-hockey player coming to the end of

his career with no future in sight
- a decent man caught up in paranormal events that terrify him
- a dying old man with much to regret
- a young mother with AIDS
- a spinster inn keeper, who sees herself as unattractive, in love with a man she thinks she will lose.

In every story (fiction) you write, you will speak with the voice of your narrator, who speaks with the voice(s) of the POV character(s).

Remember: *You* stay out of sight.

You keep back.

You never intrude or let your narrator intrude.

You let your characters act out/tell their stories.

William Hazlitt (1778-1830) an English essayist and critic put it beautifully:

The greater the artist, the deeper he will submerge himself in his material, without ramming home the moral or otherwise advertising his presence.

"Without… advertising his presence."

You are not there.
You see through somebody else's eyes.
You hear with somebody else's ears.
You touch with somebody else's hands.

You speak with somebody else's voice.

When I wrote *Red Dragon Square* I spoke with Arnold's voice. Arnold is not, like me, a sort-of-retired writing teacher-turned-Acquisitions Editor; he is a young man of limited education caught up in events he doesn't fully understand. If he ever comes across as an old school teacher, I'm cooked.

In *A Light Above the Sun* I spoke with the voice of a twelve-year-old girl.

To give myself a rest after Arnold and Daisy, I began *Hano and Star* (still unfinished) in which I speak with the voice of an old professor. That is comfortable!

Come to Say Good-Bye required me to speak with the voice of a fifty-year-old accountant, a single man who grew up on the prairies. I had to learn that voice. I knew nothing about being an accountant and have never lived on the prairies, but I think I learned to speak as Richard Waterman.

There may be more than one voice/narrator/narrative voice, especially in a long novel. *Doomsday Book* requires a voice for the fourteenth century: Kivrin, the student-historian; and one for her own time: the voice of her student advisor. Problems are not just doubled, but compounded. Connie Willis took five years to write *Doomsday Book*.

The **Common Voice Errors**, then:
1.   **Error**: Thinking you can speak with your own voice.
     Remedy: Learn the voice you need for your story.

2.   **Error**: Forgetting sometimes to speak with your required voice.
     Remedy: Be alert for slips like that and correct them.

E. Learning Your Craft

This section, too, is based on my seminar notes and applies (chiefly) to writing fiction.

Scenes

You know what scenes are: discrete pieces of a story with beginning and end of their own.

"A novel is a fictitious prose narrative of considerable length and complexity, portraying characters and presenting a sequential organization of *action and scenes*." (Random House Dictionary)

An "organization of action and scenes."

So if you don't make scenes, you're not writing novels. You're writing something else: journals, chronicles, histories (including biographies and autobiographies) but not novels;

the difference being this:

"Frankly, Scarlet, I don't give a damn."

Then Rhett told her he didn't care. (Ann Copeland)

That is, all the difference in the world.

Through scenes your Readers slip into your stories, and you catch their interest - scare them to death, make them laugh - without putting them off or boring them.

Now then, some questions and answers about making scenes:

1.   When should you make a scene?

Whenever you want to centre your Reader's mind on something that is happening.

2.   Where?

Anywhere you like. Start with a scene if you want to. Finish with one. Just make them.

3.   Who should appear in your scenes?

Your main characters.

RULE: Nothing should be allowed in a story that does not move the story forward.

ABSOLUTELY NOTHING

A Very Important Rule

4.   Which actions should you make into scenes?

The important ones. Ones that move the story forward.

5.   How long are scenes?

As long as necessary, always remembering that nothing stays in but what moves the story forward – no lecturing, preaching, or teaching.

A little girl comes onto a stage and recites:

> I am an aching void
> where loneliness resides.
> Where have you gone?
> Where have you gone?

Her parents in the audience are astounded.

That was a thirty-second TV commercial, a gem, and a complete, perfect little scene – but not a good commercial; I can't remember what it tried to sell.

Then there are scenes that go on page, after page, after page.

Scenes include:

- action
- conversation
- description
- narrative

in varying amounts

Typically they have all four, but in practice some may be missing.

Then how does a writer create a scene?

The characters move and talk.

You've learned how to make your characters move:

Be sure your Reader knows where the relevant characters are at all times.

Let the Reader share the action. (Remember Joni and her coffee.) Talking, well...

One of the criteria I use when I take my first peek at your MS is: HOW DO THE CHARACTERS SPEAK?

If they talk like TV actors, I'll know. I'll know that you haven't gone out among your friends and neighbours and listened. And that will be a big black mark against you. I'll think, *Fake!*

Writing Speech:

As a writer you have to study speech patterns *where you live*.

Have you noticed how women speak these days? Voiceless? I hope I live long enough to hear women and girls take back their voices. I could give you my sociological theory as to why women rasp unpleasantly, but I am only going for comparison here. My meaning is, like... Well, you know like, I mean, take country singers. There's a Texas drawl, like, or something, that they all have to imitate. Though they may come from the coast of Labrador, if they want to sing "country" they have to say "Ah met her in Texas and mah heart was broken." Or, as a waitress - I mean a server of the female gender - once said to my husband on a hot day in Abilene, when what he had set his heart on was a long, cold beer, "No suh, Abilene's derraihh."

Editors have special antennae in their heads. So get out and mingle. You don't have to make a special effort. You'll need bread and milk and a carton of OJ every day or so.

To make characters talk, simply put the words into their mouths that they would probably say.

1. Make them speak naturally to fit the occasion and the mood.

2. Use tags (he saids, she saids) where needed

- to show who is speaking
- to keep the rhythm flowing
- to show the manner of a character's speaking

For example, "Pete yelled."

And here's a point. Prefer "Pete yelled," to "yelled Pete." Placing the name last gives a feeling of finality that spoils the smooth flow of the story.

Note: Use verbs.

Say "Pete yelled," not "Pete said angrily."

Avoid adverbs.

3. Avoid slang; it dates your story very rapidly.

4. Be cautious of dialect; you must know it very well, and it is likely that many of your Readers will not know it. Usually a few typical words used throughout will indicate dialect and be sufficient.

Writing Narrative:

Linkage between scenes, descriptions of people and places.

Narration should be kept within strict bounds.

1. Use only what is necessary, and only what moves the story forward.

2. Resist I by N's (Intrusions by the Narrator.)

3. Let the characters experience directly whatever is to be seen, heard, or otherwise taken in.

4. If you find yourself tempted to put in long passages of reporting, stop and make a scene instead.

Example:

...and then Kenny thought he should go to the kitchen and make some supper so he did, and he found some eggs and cheese and bread, and he cooked the eggs in a pot of water, and then his sister came in and said he should turn the heat up or the eggs would never cook so he did, and, and, and...

Instead of a bunch of dead verbiage, write a scene.

Conversation:

"Wow! I'm starving," Kenny said to himself. "I wonder what there is in the house to eat. I guess Mom won't mind if I rummage around a bit."

Description:

The kitchen was warm and inviting and made him think he'd like cooking.

Conversation again:

"Guess I'll see if we have any eggs," he muttered. "I know how to cook eggs."

Narration/description:

He found a saucepan in a cupboard and put about a gallon of water in it, and two white eggs.

More conversation:

"That should be enough," he said. "Wonder what temperature Mom uses for eggs. Better not be too hot. Don't want to burn the house down…

"Should take three minutes," he reminded himself. "Time enough to call George."

More narration/description:

Half an hour later Corinna came in from school, with a bang of the back door, and dropped her bag of books on the kitchen table with a crash.

Back to conversation:

"Hey, Kenny," she yelled. "What's in the pot?"

"I'm boiling eggs," he shouted back from the phone in the living room.

"What? In that pot? How long have they been in?"

You get the idea.

NEVER BORE YOUR READER. THERE'S NO NEED.

Finally, how much description of people and places should you use?

Very little. Remember the Granny Smith apple?

As illustration:

"He was forty-six, a short stocky Lowland Scot... whose plain common sense had appealed to my uncle after the turmoil stirred up by an arrogant predecessor." (Dick Francis, *To the Hilt*)

This is enough to peg the character in the Reader's mind, and, you will notice, it moves the story forward at the same time.

If a novel is like a string of beads, the beads being scenes, how do you string them together?

With as few words as possible.

Resist the urge to write everything you know. If Scene One takes place on Monday and Scene Two on Friday, don't put in Tuesday, Wednesday, and Thursday.

When you read other writers, notice how they do it. Some make long dissertations which are generally lecturing, preaching, or teaching, and pretty boring; some jump from one scene to the next like kids playing on pans of ice. In *Deep Secret*, Diana Wynne Jones sometimes goes so far as to cut into the living flesh, as it were. She will start a scene with "...and a partial sentence." That's a bit drastic, perhaps, but shows what you can do.

Remember, brevity is a virtue. Whatever you do, don't be long-winded.

Maybe we should make that a rule. I'll borrow one from Professor Strunk:

RULE: NO UNNECESSARY WORDS. (*Elements of Style*)

All right, then, we have one common error here:

Error: Not making scenes.

Remedy: Make them.

A Word to Start You Off:

When writing your first draft, let it all gush onto the paper. ***Don't stop to think.*** I mean that. Doing first drafts, never stop to think. If a word doesn't come right along, go ahead without it; it will turn up later. If you can't spell a word, make a stab at it and correct it later. Don't answer the phone. Don't stop for drinks. Don't look around for inspiration. Just go.

Bradbury calls this burning down the house. He says,

> This afternoon burn down the house. Tomorrow pour cold
> critical water upon the smouldering coals.
> (Zen in the Art of Writing)

Zen: a mystical Japanese form of Buddhism that emphasizes contemplation
     and solitary study to achieve self-discipline and intuitive spiritual en-
     lightenment.

Pouring cold critical water is self-editing.

A few tips:

1. When cutting work to required lengths, cut words, cut narrative, cut description; never cut out scenes.

2. When you need more words, add scenes. Never pad with narrative, description, adverbs and adjectives.

3. Use verbs and nouns.

4. Be lively, never wordy.

Have fun! And make scenes all over the place. Make scenes that your Reader participates in. (Remember Joni breathing the aroma of fresh-brewed coffee.)

MAKE SCENES

      MAKE SCENES

           MAKE SCENES

Some Lessons in Lively Writing:

How to do it.

Early on a June morning Joni Plenghorn sat in her A-frame cottage looking out of the window.

Joni's house looked out on the Bay of Fundy shore where, in June, lupins bloom, along with wild roses and other flowers. The soil is thin and gravelly, but the flowers do well, like squatters taking over.

Joni had just moved to her house. She had a new table with a glass top, but no chair, so she was sitting on the edge of a packing case which cut into her bottom through her jeans. Her bare feet pressed hard against the tile floor of her house to keep the case from being too painful.

She held a mug of steaming coffee in her hands. The steam rose into her nose and made her smile.

What do you think?   Pretty lively?

If you say yes, go to the back of the class. There's not much life here. It's dull, flat, uninteresting, heavy-going, and doesn't promise to be much of anything. I for one - one of many, I'm sure - would put it back on the shelf at this point. I would not buy it - even for 99¢ in a bargain bin.

Now why is it so bad?

After all, it answers most of the questions a good beginning is supposed to answer.

Who?   Joni Plenghorn.

Where?   The Fundy shore.

When?   June.

What social conditions?

Well, this Joni appears to have her own house surrounded by flowers.

What mood?   She's smiling.

But the writing - the story-telling - does not engage the reader.

P.G. Wodehouse (pronounced Woodhouse) was a great one for saying that a story must grip - and *this one doesn't.*

Note: In case you're wondering who this P.G. Wodehouse was, and why you should listen to him, P.G. Wodehouse lived into his middle 90's and had published a book for every year of his age. He was good. He had a huge following - still does. And he knew how to grip a reader in a stranglehold and never let go.

P.G. would not approve of this story: *It does not grip.*

It does not appeal to any of the reader's interests, feelings, emotions. It is just words.

And why? *Why is this story just words?*

If you are to succeed as a writer, you must grasp the answer to this question.

You must understand it.

You must learn the secret that is written on this page, which is:

The problem with this story is that it is reported by an external narrator; it is not experienced by the reader.

Joni is described by somebody who is not one with her.

not inside her mind and body.

not sharing her emotions.

And the result is BORING.

Here's the beginning of *Blackberry Light* again.

June was "bustin' out all over."

June was bustin' out in northern sunshine and the pearly glow of early morning by the sea. It was bustin' out of the thin soil of Hamilton Harbour as tough little wild roses, and as lupin volunteering in gravelly patches as if by squatters' rights. It was bustin' out in Joni Plenghorn's A-frame cottage - threatening to bust right through the roof. And June was bustin' out in Joni Plenghorn's heart.

Joni perched on the edge of a packing crate and leaned on her new glass-topped table with both elbows, a mug of fresh-brewed coffee in her hands. Her bare toes pressed against her terra cotta floor, feeling the tiles warm and rough and earthy. Her knees and thighs received the same solid pressure, and exulted in it. Through worn old denim the packing crate cut into her bottom, but her spine and shoulders met the need with pleasure, and the back of her neck felt the push of the floor as if it had been the lift in her heart. Coffee aroma filled the air she breathed, and she smiled, a slow, supremely happy smile from deep inside her soul.

The difference is in the narrator. The teller of this version is inside Joni - mind, heart, and whole body.

And again:

Try this.

Islands in a Bay is a "romance" about a woman who runs a country inn on the Bay of Fundy and a school teacher from Ontario who comes to stay at the inn.

Are you going to buy the book?

Phone-in poll results:

Yes: 1%   No: 99%

Yet this is how many stories (mostly unpublished) begin.

Now add a few details to the picture:

Islands in a Bay is a romance about a long, gangly woman who runs a country inn on the Fundy shore near Saint John and a teacher of physics at a private school in Ontario who comes to stay at the inn.

Results of poll:

Yes: 15-20%   No: 60%   Undecided: 20-25%

Try again:

Vi Gables runs Inn on the Cliff near Saint John, New Brunswick. Lionel Leonard, a teacher of physics in Ontario, comes to stay at the inn.

Results:

Back to about one buyer in every hundred browsers.

Oh. Well:

Islands in a Bay is a romance about Vi Gables, a long, gangly woman who runs the Inn on the Cliff on the Fundy shore. Lionel Leonard, also long and gangly, comes to stay at the inn. Love at first sight!

Here maybe the yes vote will go up to 25 or 30%.

Probably not.

Now put some zing into this story:

Vi Gables - tall, gangly, and pushing forty - runs the Inn on the Cliff. Vi spends her free time secretly writing adventure stories about a gorgeous "Rawshun" called Feodor Lofcenko.

Lionel Leonard - tall, gangle, and never going to see fifty again - comes to stay at the Inn. Lionel spends his free time writing torrid romances about a girl called Launie Lawrence.

This is better, but a story like this is never going to succeed if it starts out with narration/explanation. Jump right in. Make a scene.

Islands in a Bay
Chapter 1

Vi Gables, owner-manager, Inn-on-the-Cliff (B&B; dinner by arrangement) heard the latest honeymoon couple coming downstairs and checked her smile in the mirror behind the kitchen door. Vi hated honeymoon couples.

"Typical," she muttered. "Everyone else up and gone. Long since about their business. But these two... If only there weren't so many weddings. If there weren't so many blasted honeymoons. If Inn-on-the-Cliff weren't such a romantic setting. Well, I wrote the brochure myself, so what can I expect. But if only honeymooners didn't provide so much of my income..."

"Lookink good, Wi," Feodor drawled.

"Yes?" she drawled back. "Me? Or the strawberries?"

"Darlink," Feodor protested, lounging from the corner by the sink toward the berry dishes, "Ivan Feodorovich, as you wery well know, eats r-red meat. R-r-red meat, darlink, with plenty of wodka - and a bowl of borscht when Wi insist."

"I know," Vi replied with a sigh. "And don't bother to cook the meat."

Feodor scooped a finger through a dish of strawberries and licked off the juice he picked up. His mouth curled, downward.

"It is a wonder, Wi," he said, "that you have any *but* honeymoon couples comink to your inn. A man in his right minds... Now in Rawsha..."

"Never mind. I know all about Rawsha," Vi snapped. "Stand out of my way, you oaf. My guests are down and will doubtless remember, eventually, that they have come expecting breakfast."

She arranged her smile for the third time - Feodor's appearances in the kitchen always wiped it away - and marched into the sun porch.

"Good-morning, Mr. James," she said to the bridegroom. "Good-morning, my dear," to the bride. "I hope you found your accommodation to your liking?"

"Oh, yes. Very," they both replied with wide smiles, as if they had been waiting for an excuse to smile widely - as they probably had. And Mrs. James went on to remark upon the fine day and Vi's beautiful view over the bay and the islands.

"Yes, isn't it," Vi replied, without even thinking.

"We're going for a nice long walk," Mrs. James added, and twinkled at her husband, who beamed at her.

"Just like a man with a idiot child what recites Dostoevski by the heart," Feodor remarked.

He was standing with his back against the glass wall that looked out over the bay, and the islands, and the beautiful morning.

"Feodor," Vi snarled, "vamoose, you bloody Rawshun. Remove yourself. How many times do I have to tell you?"

He leered and loped off toward the side door to the garden.

"Darlink," he drawled, just before he banged the screen behind him, "Darlink Wi, you are so cute when you are angry."

"Oh, for God's sake!" Vi muttered.

"...if there are birds to be seen nearby... My wife is passionately fond of..."

"Passionately," Feodor carolled through the screen. "Send them up the old planting ground along the road, Wi. Wery passionate places, planting grounds. Back in Rawsha..."

"Oh, yes, we have lots of birds," Vi told the new Jameses. "Most of our shore birds have moved on, of course. But if you aren't afraid of old cemeteries and have brought stout shoes, the boundary bushes are full of nesting songbirds - robins, sparrows, warblers..."

"Perfect," Mrs. James cooed. "We are passionately fond of warblers, aren't we, Kenneth."

Mr. James beamed.

Feodor gave Mr. James thumbs up, winked at Vi, and jumped over the cliff to the beach.

"Good," Vi said to herself. "Gone swimming. Now if I can get these turtle doves off to the graveyard, I'll maybe squeeze in a minute or two at the word processor before..."

Poll results now?

Yes: 98%   No: 2% (sour pusses who can't stand silliness.)

Beginnings in Summary

> "They shoot the white girl first."
>
> (Toni Morrison, *Paradise*)

BEGINNINGS SHOULD GRIP.

Sometimes the narrator begins:

Narrator beginnings may grip and hold the Reader, as Jane Austen did with her ironic pronouncement about "a truth universally acknowledged."

Or they may become a laughing stock, like poor old Buller-Lytton's "It was a dark and stormy night."

Sometimes the characters begin a story with a scene. That's usually good.

But whatever way you choose to begin, grip your Reader pronto: non-gripping results in a story non-read. (You don't have to be aggressive about this gripping, just strong.)

Resist the temptation to – you know – lecture, preach, or teach.

Do not suppose that you have to sit down with your Reader and say, "Now, before we can begin, I have to tell you that this story takes place in… in the year…　　Mrs. Character is a woman in her…　　's married to… with…　　children. She has…"

No, no, no. Never, never, never. *You* may sit down to explain all this, but I'll bet your Reader won't. And I *know* that if I were your editor, *I* wouldn't.

No, no. **Beginnings should grip!**

Beginnings should grip from inside the story and drag your Reader into the story.

Beginnings should have your Reader bug-eyed in the first paragraph.

Avoid; at all costs avoid going back into the past to explain about what used to go on. Avoid. Avoid. Avoid.
Example, *bad*:

Mary Lynn stepped off the bus at her corner. It had been a long day.

She had overslept because her alarm had not rung. She had skipped break-fast and that had brought on an attack of indigestion. She had gone to the drugstore, etc. etc. etc.

By now you must have seen what happened here. In the first sentence, you *were* Mary Lynn. You were stepping off the bus with her. Besides, you had the advantage of not knowing what was coming next; it could have been fun! But no. Along comes this prosy, negative-thinking, boring old external narrator. "Boring" is a **BAD** word!

No, no. If you need all this stuff about Mary Lynn's day, say some-thing like this:

Mary Lynn stepped off the bus at her corner. The knot in her stomach from waking up late and skipping breakfast was gone...

Here, no boring narrator. The author stays with Mary Lynn *in her present time* and lets her work her way through the story.

Note: The bad parts of her day are *subordinated*. If you know the language of grammar, you will see that they have been relegated to a phrase:
"from waking up late and skipping breakfast."

A phrase is a lesser member of the construction crew. The sentence is the boss; phrases are only part-time helpers. In the first, the boring version of this tale, all the ho-hum facts were made into sentences. They never should have been. They should have been whittled down into *subordinate* parts and added as needed - if needed. Think of subordinates as those little pieces of wood and "stuff" that collect on building sites. Builders sometimes rummage through piles of them when they are looking for a bit of this or that, but most of them are shovelled into dumpsters when the job is finished.

Now listen:

The above advice applies equally to background material about the whole lives of your characters that you may think essential. It may be essential, but never resort to:

She had been born in Florida. Her mother had come from England. Her father had been born in Zambia and had been educated in London...

No, no, no! Subordinate! Each fact will come out if it's important.

You can talk about "her English mother" - the whole sentence about her mother is then subordinated to the level where it belongs; it has shrunk to one word, and that's a helping word, an adjective. And it is not going to bore your reader.

> **If you find yourself writing whole passages in the past perfect, "had" tense, you need to review this section.**

And while we're at it, *never* use the past perfect tense when you need the simple past. Many people nowadays make this mistake. They think they're being correct. They're not. If you are talking about something that happened yesterday, do not use "had".

Yesterday I saw a bald eagle.

Never, Yesterday I had seen a bald eagle.

Unless. Unless there is a time difference in the past to explain. As, Yesterday I saw a bald eagle *after* I had seen a golden eagle.

The "had" tense is for going back farther into the past. Use it only for that purpose.

If you say,

Yesterday I had seen a bald eagle after I had seen a golden eagle,

you're not making sense.

I hope you can comprehend the distinction. If not, you had better round up some books from middle school and get to work. "Had" may be little but she's mighty, and her strangle hold on our language is strong.

For this reason I also advise against prefaces, forewords, and introductions. Let the beginning of the story fill in the when and where, the situations and the background. Let the characters reveal the details by what they say and do. You keep out of it.

Beginnings have to accomplish a great deal, though:

- make clear when and where
- introduce the *main* characters
- provide the general geographical and social milieu of the story
- set the tone or mood of the story.

A word about Tone/Mood

Tone/Mood (the same for our purposes) is the general "feel" of the story; how it makes the Reader feel: happy, amused, angry, fearful, irritated...

I wonder where this tone or mood comes from! Maybe we should have discussed it under theme. Are you now beginning to understand the importance of theme?

Never let theme out of your mind, and you'll have no trouble maintaining the tone or mood of your story; it will be automatic.

On this point, you may stroke the chicken's feathers a little if you want to. A sizzling romance can weary if the characters never simmer down. A story of loss and grief can overwhelm without occasional relief. You will remember from school hearing of comic relief – Shakespeare often used it in his sombre plays. But overall, maintain the mood you start with.

Maintain the mood you start with. That's the main point about mood/tone. Carry on as you begin. Don't start dancing a jig right after the funeral, unless you have a compelling reason to do so.

Now, Writing Beginnings:

You may spend a lot of time on your first page or two. But don't try to do this work all at once, or even when you begin to write the story. Let the beginning evolve. You may change your mind a dozen times before you're through.

You're going to burn down the house first, remember. But the fire will never catch if you try to find the perfect beginning from day one. In fact, when you come next day to pour "cold critical water" on your "smouldering coals," you'll often find that your story really starts on p4 or p5. Don't spare the delete key; get rid of 1, 2, and 3.

Some general comments:

Even a short novel, of course, is 50,000 words and takes time to accomplish. You'd have to burn down the whole town if you did your rough draft all at once and never looked back. No, you can't do that, but you can burn down the house each time you write a new part.

Hemingway used to write a section today. Then tomorrow he would read through the first pages, doing a little light editing to be sure he was on track (remember theme) before going on to new stuff. Until the story became too long, he would read it all before starting to write. After that he would go back a couple of chapters or so each day. I find his system works for me. You may like it too.

So, Errors around Beginnings:

1.   **Error**: No, I won't say it again: l., p. and t.

      Remedy: Jump right into the story.

2.   **Error**: Thinking, "I can't begin; therefore I can't write."

      Remedy: Nonsense!

3.   **Error**: Trying to write the beginning first.

      Remedy: Finalize the beginning when you are sure how the story is going to progress and end.

This advice applies to titles too. Working titles help you to talk about your story, and you need one for your headers, but final titles often come just before a book goes to the printer.

ALLISON SAYS:

TITLES

WHAT'S IN A NAME?

What you call your literary offspring is important. In contrast to the name you choose for your child, your book needs a unique caption: a favorite appellation you've repeatedly heard will not do.

Not only should your book have a distinctive title - one which singles it out and captures the attention of a would-be reader at a glance, intriguing him - it must also be an accurate key to the contents.

As well, your title needs to be short - a few words, maybe only one, which will not only rivet the attention of a prospective reader but will fit handily on the cover, leaving room for the viewer to take in the cover illustration at the same time.

Sound easy? After all, you may say to yourself, it's only a matter of coming up with a very few words. A snap?... Not necessarily.

You may have fixed on a title you love even before you begin your book. Sometimes it will turn out to be just right; sometimes not. Keep an open mind.

For instance, it is possible to decide on a title you are sure is original only to learn that about a dozen other people have come to the same conclusion. I once decided that First Person Singular was an apt and catchy title for a collection I'd written from a first person point of view. Fortunately, I asked my daughter Stephanie, to check on Amazon.com to see if, by chance, any other writers had used the same title. They had: Joyce Carol Oates and about ten others.

Obviously, I had to come up with a new title. Although I was initially unhappy about this turn of events, the title I eventually decided on was much better for my collection, thus proving to be the proverbial blessing in disguise.

Anyway, my warning is: before your book goes off to the editor of your choice, make sure that your title is both unique and appropriate.

NOW: Some *How To*:

Much about craft runs through *all* Allison and I are telling you, and I couldn't possibly tell you even all *I* know about craft in the time we have. All I can do is pass on to you a few sparks of the fire I have warmed at in my editing practice.

For the rest:

- Read for style and technique, not just for content.
- Study punctuation (practice keeps changing)
    - spelling (don't rely on your computer to know)
    - sentence structure
    - paragraphing
    - dividing into chapters
    - how other people handle action, grief, panic, sex…

We have already discussed choices writers make for euphony, to make the work suit the subject and the mood of the writing. Here's where that lesson applies.

When writing

Action:

To hold your reader, would you say:

My son was sheer poetry in action in his hockey game last night. He came out of the players' box like a young gazelle, and having taken possession of the puck, stick-handled his way past all opposing players and found himself confronting the visitors' goaltender who...

You start telling that story in the office, and unless you're the boss, you'll be alone in about fifteen seconds.

No. No. Say:

Jamie stormed over the boards and hit the ice at 100 klicks. You should have seen him grab the puck away from young Percival and start down the ice with it. It was beautiful. That poor goalie on the other team just stood there with his mouth open.

Short, sharp, active words.

Sentences that rush to conclusion.

Vivid word pictures of energy, speed, dexterity, and consternation in the ranks of the opposition.

You achieve life in your writing by your choice of words; in action, especially verbs.

Portraying grief, you would do the opposite.

Tears gathered in Alice's eyes, and slowly welled over her eyelids and slid down her cheeks. She didn't seem to notice. She sank onto the bedside of her dying child and reached for his poor, thin little hand.

You can pour on this stuff till your reader is weeping with Alice, tear for tear. But don't carry any technique too far, or your reader will begin to snicker; your story will have ceased to grip.

Moderation in all things.

Every human emotion requires its own approach. Each fictional experience of that emotion requires its own intensity, its own degree of involvement of the reader. There are no hard and fast rules; there's only what happens when *you* bring your *style* to the description of any situation.

The point is that you must *deal* with emotions to write good fiction.

Do not stand back and report. Jump right in there. Leap over the boards with Jamie. Weep with Alice. *DO IT.*

- Don't copy other writers, but use what's useful to you of their methods and techniques.
- Love words
- Write every day for the hell of it.

Plot:

My usual comment on first reading a MS is, "You have a good story here, but it needs work."

It needs work because you wrote it not knowing the concepts we have been discussing.

The point about plot is:

Don't make it up; write it down (Julia Cameron.)

That is, let the story develop on its own. Keep a tight rein only on theme.

Plot is how you illustrate your theme.

Plot needs people (characters) and conflict (not necessarily aggression, but a problem to solve) against a background (setting.) When these come together, a story happens.

RULE: **Shout down your own well and see what comes up.**

Characters:

> "Find a character, like yourself, who will
> want something or not want something, with
> all his heart. Give him running orders. Shoot
> him off. Then follow as fast as you can go."
> (Bradbury)

Introduce your main characters first.

Do not add characters after your story is well started, unless you're writing historical novels. Even so, try to tie everything together.

Avoid stereotypes. Make your characters one of a kind.

You will hear of round and flat characters.

Round characters are important, main characters; those who have to be known, warts and all, to the readers.

Spend time developing the personalities of these characters, BUT make sure that essential physican facts about them are established in the first time they appear.

That is, if Alicia's red hair or Roland's flat feet need to be known, make sure the reader has the information when she begins forming her mental picture of this character. Readers hate to be told, half way through a story, that a girl they had pictured little and cute weighs three hundred pounds and has a face like a turkey gobbler.

Flat characters are those, less important to the reader, who may be pictured any old which-way, because nobody cares what they look like, and the reader has to know only that they are reliable, or unreliable - or something like that.

That is, you should not waste words describing, even naming, a character who appears only once or twice. And never mind Old Grandma if her only characteristic is that she's bad tempered. She can stay flat.

When you read *Doomsday Book*, notice how Connie Willis handles the character of the village priest. At first she allows him to be a slightly sinister figure. But when he dies of plague on the floor of his church, the last of the villagers to succumb, having buried the forty others, strong men take off their glasses and wipe their eyes. When you have forgotten everything else about that book, you will remember Father Roch.

Note: Describe heroes of romances – they're all tall, dark, and handsome. But don't describe the heroines – because your Reader is a woman and knows what she's like.

Make sure your characters speak naturally. On this point,

- if you're going to write about a time in the past, clear out of your vocabulary words and expressions not in common use at the time. Read some of Georgette Heyer's Regency Romances and notice how at ease she is with the speech of the early nineteenth century.
- avoid slang; it will date your work and spoil it.
- be cautious of dialect. Use dialect only if you are perfectly familiar with it, and then only if you think your Reader is too. Often all you need is a word or two, used consistently throughout, to indicate dialect.

Setting:

Establish place and time right away, page one.

My advice: Unless you are writing fantasy, don't set a novel in a place
                  where you haven't lived for at least a full year.

Even if you are making up your place, if it's on Earth, stick to true grographical
concepts. See *Red Dragon Square*.

If you are writing out of present time, research, research, research.
Know your place and time.

Now finally, **Style**:

People often ask me about style; they seem vague about what it is.

Style is your personal stamp on everything about you.

Your writing style is your personal stamp upon your work, so make sure you
use your own style, not a borrowed one.

Your style will develop, but it will not change; you will be known by it.

You don't have to stick to your style; it will stick to you.

Style is *not* method. It's very important to keep the two separate.

You may write gothic style, western style, urban style stories – what have
you – these are all methods. Your personal style will still be stamped upon
them.

Howard, for example, writes he-man style adventure stories. Martha writes in the sugary style of the romance writers of the 1950s.

The other night I watched a "Gothic-type" movie. You know the kind: a big old house without neighbours, tensions in the house, and an innocent young girl who arrives to be housekeeper, or nanny, or something.

Only it wasn't. It wasn't Gothic - even a type of Gothic. Or it shouldn't have tried to be. Because it wasn't the girl's story at all; it was the story of the father and son who lived in the house.

The result of this mistake was that about half the length of the film was taken up with the characters sitting around in the house telling each other all about the painful things that had happened to them in the past. Very dull. That movie would have been much more interesting if those scenes from the past had been presented as they happened, but that would have made the men the main characters and the story could not have been told from the girl's POV. No more Gothic.

Watch for things like that in your own writing, and never force a story into a form it doesn't fit.

These variants of novel writing are *called* styles. But they, too, are really methods. I like to reserve the word "style" for what makes each of us, and our work, unique and identifiable.

So now you want to know: after all this, how in the world can I write an original story?

As Allison says, it isn't easy but you can learn to do it. Active verb *learn*. You have to practice, practice, practice till you can do it with your eyes shut. Well, almost!

Bradbury says
Style + Theme = Originality.
             Equal.

That means:

Theme: Writing about the things *you* love, hate, fear with a passion (theme)

      Style: with *your personal stamp* (style) upon them will result in original stories.

If you write about something
      you love
      you hate
      you fear
and if you go deep enough into both your theme and yourself, you will bring your own style to bear, and what you create will be original because there is only one you; you are unique.

You are unique; so is your work.

How this process works:

Let's say you fear spiders. You really hate the way their legs bend and lift their bulbous bodies above the ground. But you love spider webs strung with beads of dew on summer mornings.

Your story about spiders will probably tell how you ran for your life this morning when you were in your garden admiring the webs on the cabbages and one of the manufacturers walked over your bare foot.

Also, let's say you see the bright side of everything. You see the world in bright colours, you "get" the joke, you hear music in the wind, you love the harmony of placement...

Your nature will show through the story as your style. It will make the story funny, full of sunshine, bright with the green of the cabbages, the sparkle of the webs, the blue of the sky. When the spider walks over your foot, your reader will laugh. Because you're you.

There is therefore no excuse.

You *can* learn to write original stories that grip the reader and play upon his/her heart and mind.

There is no excuse. No excuse in the world.

Note: For goodness' sake:

If you don't like *his or her* all the time, don't substitute *they*.

Please make sense. Write either

...grip the reader and play upon his or her heart...

or ...grip the readers and play upon their hearts...

How can anybody in possession of an ounce of logic write:

...grip the reader and play upon their heart...

when reader (singular) and their (plural) are one and the same!

ALLISON SAYS:

ORIGINALITY

Originality stems from telling things as they are - that is, things as they are as you see them.

Sound easy? Well, I think not, since a great many people are to a considerable extent governed by what the most-in-vogue pundits have to say, as well as being in thrall to the latest fads. Some even persuade themselves that subscribing to the current extreme point of view or fad - particularly just after it has been launched - is a testament to originality.

Such attitudes, however, do not constitute originality. Originality is individuality, and because everyone differs at least slightly from everyone else and has experiences which are his or hers alone, each person has the capacity to tell what he or she knows from experiences and perceptions which are unique.

But doing this is not as easy as it might sound. Individuality needs to be cultivated as much as a garden. It takes a lot of careful digging into one's own state of mind and experiences to approach the truth as one understands it.

Honesty is the key, but achieving absolute - or near absolute - honesty is difficult. From time to time at least, we all fool ourselves by believing that what we say, often without much thought, is the exact truth. Reflection often indicates that this is not so.

Adults, by and large, have learned to monitor and adjust the truth - often without even realizing what they are doing - to fit particular social situations. Young children, by contrast, tend to come right out with what they think or observe. And so it happens that adults marvel at the freshness of the young child's utterances, and educators especially mourn the frequent loss of this originality when the child enters a conventional school system - although they tend to contribute to this loss.

This is not to say that adults should act like young children and say whatever first comes into their heads. Still, those who are driven to create need to preserve and cultivate their original perceptions. As Ralph Waldo Emerson has remarked, a person "should learn to detect and watch that gleam of light which flashes across his mind from within..." - and he should make special use of these flashes of insight since they are, when well recorded, what make for originality of expression.

So, you say, I have all these ideas which seem to be mine alone, but who, you ask, is going to be interested in what I think and feel? From experience, I would reply that you would be surprised how frequently feelings and experiences you decide to record are echoed in the hearts and minds of others. It is the adept writer who triggers these mutual responses. In so doing, he communicates well with his readers. A creative writer and a creative reader make a whole.

The famous French writer Chateaubriand has said; "The original writer is not he who refrains from imitating others, but he who can be imitated by none." And English writer-philosopher John Stuart Mill has even gone so far as to insist that "All good things which exist are the fruits of originality."

STYLE

Unfortunately, having original perceptions is not enough for the writer. It's how he or she phrases these insights that counts as well. If a writer's style is unclear or tedious, most readers, understandably, are going to put aside the story, poem or essay they have tried, unsuccessfully, to fathom. Very likely they will never pick up that discarded piece again.

Thus clarity is of first importance. The novice

writer sometimes thinks that an easy-to-read style is a sign of simple-mindedness and that he must therefore strive for a certain complexity to demonstrate his mental prowess. Besides, he supposes that achieving a free-flowing, comprehensible and expressive style is a snap.

Paradoxically, such an apparently simple style is not usually arrived at with the ease the uninitiated might imagine. It takes a considerable amount of work and a lot of self-criticism as well, to cut out the inessential verbiage obstructing the flow; to put down, as nearly as possible, exactly what you want to say.

One of the hurdles in such an attempt is that the new writer often imagines that an unbridgeable gap exists between the spoken word and the written word. I have had students whose spoken language was vital, entertaining and to the point, but who, when they put pen to paper, could not begin to duplicate such qualities. Puzzling indeed!

What I have always told would-be writers who suffer from such a discrepancy between their spoken and written language is that they should try to write their story - or whatever they want to put down on paper - as they would tell it orally. Sound simple? Yes it does, but it apparently isn't. It gen-

erally takes a lot of practice before such people can
satisfactorily translate their spoken language into
writing of the same caliber.

To achieve clarity and vitality of style, analogies are important. In our daily life most of us
naturally use analogies or comparisons to explain
more clearly and colorfully something we have
seen or heard. We want to make an impact on our
listener, want to make sure he understands and
pays attention to what we have to say - want to
entertain him too, if we can.

Yet although analogies are so significant a
part of everyday verbal communications, surpris-
ingly, would-be writers tend to eliminate such vital comparisons from their writing - or work in
ones which are inappropriate and do not ring true.

A writer famous both for the clarity of his style
and the colorful effectiveness of his analogies is
Stephan Crane. His story "The Open Boat" is often
cited as a model. His analogies such as "patches of
brown seaweed that rolled over the waves with a
movement like carpets on a line in a gale," or "it
is easier to steal eggs from under a hen than ... to
change seats in the dinghy" hit home - at least
they do for someone as old as I am, a person familiar with the sight of carpets airing on a clothes-
line and with the tricky and hazardous task of

removing eggs from under a broody hen. However, for a lot of today's young and middle-aged, such comparisons are not a part of their experience, thus having a diminished contemporary significance. From this realization, one must conclude that today's writer's images must come from the contemporary world so that his readers can relate to them readily.

Section F: Conclusions Summaries and Oops, I Forgots!

Here I'll tell you one of the tricks of my trade:

Look at dialogue.

When a MS lands on my desk, I take a peek. I read a page or two here and there. I can't resist a new MS, and the first peek almost always tells me whether or not the rest is going to be worth my time as a publisher's editor. I have to decide quickly, and the note you receive from me, saying that your MS has arrived safely, may give you a clue as to what my final decision is going to be. If I am not very encouraging, that is because I am not encouraged.

I have asked you to send your MS and I will read it. If I don't read it all, I will skim it. And if I skim, that will be because I have seen before the end that it

- is unsuitable for DreamCatcher
- needs a great deal of work because you don't yet know how to write, and I haven't enough time to teach you.

Blocking:

If the book editor thinks that rewriting is not necessary but that some pretty extensive revisions need to be made, she'll look for:

Shape:

How is your MS for shape?

Beginning - Middle - End

Build up to a climax - Denouement

Theme:

Is the theme clear?

Does the story stick to its theme?

Narrative Voice:

Are there I by Ns? That is, do you, the author, keep out of sight, or are you constantly shoving in your personal two cents' worth?

Point of View:

Is your narrator consistent, or does the POV slide from character to character?

At this point the editor will send your MS to you with her recommendations and specific directions for your guidance as you revise.

Fine-tuning:

Once revisions have been accomplished to the editor's satisfaction and yours, the fine-tuning begins:

- Are your characters always true to the natures you want them to convey to your readers?
- Do the characters speak naturally?
- Is the writing tight enough?
- Are all your statements of fact accurate?

Note: Both Allison and I have stressed accuracy. That is,

- if we writers use names of real people, we should spell them correctly.
- if we use historical facts, we should be accurate, in so far as *facts* are known.
- if we use geographical facts, we should be accu-

rate.

- even if we are making up the geography of our setting, we should make sure it follows the laws of
physics.

Check reference texts, including up-to-date maps. And think what you are saying.

Perhaps **THINK** is the most important advice we can give you.

The other night a news channel ran an article on craters that are evidence of large asteroids having struck this planet in times past. When I heard that that item was coming up, I rang my daughter, who teaches geology. I thought she would like to see the satellite photos, which, the announcer said, had just been made available for public viewing.

My daughter called me right back, laughing and groaning. "Why do we work so hard?" she wanted to know. "Why do we take our work seriously and try to do it well when we have been dead for 65,000,000 years?"

We agreed that, under the circumstances, we might as well go to the beach. Why not? That news reader, with a straight face, had claimed that the asteroid that struck the Yucatan 65,000,000 years ago *wiped out all life on Earth*. As the kids say, "Go figure."

The point of my telling this story is this: if a writer shows such obvious carelessness, thoughtlessness, or ignorance once, can we believe anything else he or she says?

You don't want to be caught out like that.

Copy-editing:

Finally, when all changes have been made, you and your editor must go over the MS once more looking for:

- spelling errors or inconsistencies (*okay* and *OK*,

for example)

- word choices that may not be the best for the specific purpose of a passage, or for the target readership
- punctuation
- name changes.

Believe it or not, the names of your characters will sometimes change in your mind, or you will purposely change them. Take care. You will forget.

CONCLUSION

I have been pretty hard on you, haven't I: stay out of your own stories, keep your oar out of this stream, nobody wants you. That's because I have to reverse many of your ideas about your identity as a novelist. I hope I have succeeded in that.

I hope you see now that, as Julia Cameron puts it, your function as a novelist is not to think things up but to take things down.

And I hope you see that the function of a novel is not to stand alone but to stand for the loves, hates, and fears that, in Bradbury's metaphor, you have called up from the deep well of your being.

I think it a fine thing to be a novelist, published or not; if you have created a novel, you are a novelist. Be proud of that. Of course we all hope to be published, but writing is creation and publishing is business; and between the two is a great gulf fixed. Never think little of yourself if you have not crossed that gulf. The day may come. We do not fail as writers till we give up writing.

Bernie Siegel says,
> "You may live six years and die knowing who you are.
> Or you may die at ninety-six still rehearsing."

Always keep in mind the three requirements of a work of art: Clarity, Unity, Euphony

Suggestions for Books you Need:

1. A comprehensive, up-to-date dictionary, American or British

2. A Canadian dictionary (optional)

3. A good thesaurus - Roget's probably

Note: I still don't trust computer programs to be always accu-
          rate and/or acceptable; keep the books too.

4. A good writer's guidebook to style and usage.

   The classic is Strunk and White, *Elements of Style*

   And if you are lucky enough to find an old schoolbook called *Mastering Effective English*, hold onto it.

   Otherwise, any good guidebook. Publishers keep pumping them out every year. Ask a teacher or professor of English Lit.

5. A few encouraging books on the writing life.

   I suggest   Ray Bradbury, *Zen in the Art of Writing*
                 Julia Cameron, *The Right to Write* and *Walking in This World*

                 Stephen King, *On Writing*

AND NEVER BORE YOUR READER.

The members of that library book club I mentioned each took away several new novels from each meeting. At the following meeting they reported to the librarian what they thought. Most, *and I mean MOST*, of those books - all of them new novels that had gone through the publishing process - were never finished by those readers. Typical of their remarks:

- I read about a hundred pages but couldn't get into it.
- I didn't really read it all. I couldn't figure out what she was talking about.
- No, I didn't like this one. He insulted my intelligence. As if I wouldn't know what a slime fish was without some man lecturing me on it!
- Ah, no. Bor-r-ring.

NEVER BORE YOUR READER.

ALLISON SAYS:

No one in his right mind would consider building a house without having a solid foundation in place, yet a surprising number of people ignore the fact that writing needs just as firm and careful a base and logical plan.

A colorful and imaginative use of words, analogies which strike sympathetic chords in the reader, taking writer and reader far beyond the basics, is usually the product of a lot of experience and thoughtful insights. Not everyone who writes or even gets published manages to reach this distinctive stage. A flair for really original expression is something which cannot be learned in a classroom. It is, I suspect, a God-given gift.

Or, as P.G. Wodehouse once said:

"It was one of the dullest speeches I ever heard. The Agee woman told us for three quarters of an hour how she came to write her beastly book, when a simple apology was all that was required."

The Girl in Blue
1960

The Expert Amateur

Are you the Amateur Expert
		the Expert Amateur?
Do you have your favourite author models? Do you quote them to your editor? Do you tell her how *they* do things? By implication, that they do things better than she does?
Well,
They are not here. She is.
They are not your editor. She is.
They know nothing about you. She does.

Are you full of compliments? Do you tell your editor that she is a wonderful, knowledgeable, helpful teacher/editor, but... Is the *but* always there; unstated but there?
Remember,
You have a special friend in your editor.
She does teach her writers.
She does know what she is talking about.
Her models are as good as yours.
You are lucky to have her; you won't get them.

Are you adversarial and smarmy at the same time? Do you believe you have to establish dominance in the relationship?
Remember,
The editor has the last word.
She can cut you off at the pass and lose nothing; you have everything to lose.
She is the Expert Professional
		the Professional Expert.

This book is a gift to aspiring writers and to published writers as well. Would-be-published authors will find it a well of usefulness. Those who have been through the mill already will find much to chuckle over. Allison and Yvonne share the joy they find in writing, and teaching writers, to write better, along with the practical wisdom they have gathered in their pursuit of the writing life.

I was very pleased when these two women, my writers as well as my friends, agreed to undertake this project. It is unlike both of them to hold forth about their accomplishments, but I think they have enjoyed putting this project together.

This book does not follow the usual pattern of writers' handbooks. *The Editor Makes House Calls* deals with many aspects of good writing that are not ordinarily covered in books for beginners: aspects like the importance of sticking to your theme, how to create atmosphere, how to avoid saying too much, how to avoid boring your readers, how to reach out from inside a story and hook your reader in.

It deals, as well, with how to approach and talk with publishers, who really have the upper hand – in two ways: they have the last word on what they publish and when and how they publish it, and they *always* have far more manuscripts offered than they will ever be able to accept.

It's a publisher's world. Those writers do best who find out what publishers want before approaching them, and who approach them with some knowledge of how they work, and who look as if they can be team players.

This book contains many examples of how to write well, of how to maintain professional demeanour, and how to keep your name before the public.

The writers of *The Editor Makes House Calls* join me in offering encouragement and practical help to the many talented writers I meet as a book publisher, and to the multitudes of others who never reach my office door because their work is not good enough to get by the editor's desk.

If you want to write, write. But learn how first. Never give up. There is no such thing as Writers' Block; there are only excuses. And cream does rise to the top, given time, hard word, and perseverance.

Elizabeth Margaris
Publisher
DreamCatcher Publishing, Inc.
Saint John, New Brunswick

About the Authors

Yvonne Wilson is the editor-in-chief of DreamCatcher Publishing and a novelist. Allison Mitcham is the author of 30 books (poetry, non-fiction and fiction), as well as many poems and articles which have appeared in numerous magazines and periodicals throughout Canada and the United States. Both Wilson and Mitcham have presided over writing classes, edited books and been instrumental in launching other writers. Based on her personal experience, Wilson has conducted useful and popular seminars for writers and would-be writers on subjects such as "How to Impress a Publisher's Book Editor" - one of the topics she discusses in this volume.

The Editor Makes House Calls, a book requested by Elizabeth Margaris, publisher of DreamCatcher, in response to many queries, covers a multitude of topics having to do with writing and editing and stems from the first-hand experience of both Wilson and Mitcham.

Order Form

The Editor Makes House Calls: ISBN: 1-894372-26-3
    Secrets of Being Published $24.95 CAN $20.00 US
    Mitcham & Wilson

Other Mitcham titles

Maritime Voices   ISBN: 1-894372-06-9
                                     $19.95 CAN $15.00 US

Strange Lights at Midnight   ISBN: 1-894372-13-1
                                     $18.95 CAN $15.00 US

Angels in the Snow   ISBN: 1-9664476-1-1
                                     $12.95 CAN $9.00 US

Other Wilson titles

Red Dragon Square   ISBN: 1-894372-03-4
                                     $19.95 CAN $15.00 US

A Light Above the Sun   ISBN: 1-894372-10-7
                                     $12.95 CAN $9.00 US

Come to Say Good-Bye   ISBN: 1-894372-20-4
                                     $18.95 CAN $14.00 US

Add 7% GST in New Brunswick   _____

Shipping and Handling
(add $4.00 for single copy;   _____
 $2.00 for each additional copy)

TOTAL   _____

QUICKFAX or   DreamCatcher Publishing
e-mail your order: Suite 306, Dockside, 1 Market Square
Fax: (506) 632-4009   Saint John, NB, Canada E2L 4Z6
E-mail: dcpub@fundy.net   WebSite: www.dreamcatcher.nb.ca

MEMBER OF SCABRINI MEDIA

Quebec, Canada
2003